FRIENDSHIP AND LOVE

THE ENCYCLOPEDIA OF
HEALTH

THE LIFE CYCLE

Dale C. Garell, M.D. · General Editor

FRIENDSHIP AND LOVE

Rebecca Stefoff

Introduction by C. Everett Koop, M.D., Sc.D.
Surgeon General, U.S. Public Health Service

CHELSEA HOUSE PUBLISHERS
New York   Philadelphia

The goal of the ENCYCLOPEDIA OF HEALTH *is to provide general information in the ever-changing areas of physiology, psychology, and related medical issues. The titles in this series are not intended to take the place of the professional advice of a physician or other health-care professional.*

Chelsea House Publishers
EDITOR-IN-CHIEF: Nancy Toff
EXECUTIVE EDITOR: Remmel T. Nunn
MANAGING EDITOR: Karyn Gullen Browne
COPY CHIEF: Juliann Barbato
PICTURE EDITOR: Adrian G. Allen
ART DIRECTOR: Maria Epes
MANUFACTURING MANAGER: Gerald Levine

The Encyclopedia of Health
SENIOR EDITOR: Sam Tanenhaus

Staff for FRIENDSHIP AND LOVE
ASSISTANT EDITOR: Laura Dolce
DEPUTY COPY CHIEF: Ellen Scordato
EDITORIAL ASSISTANT: Jennifer Trachtenberg
PICTURE RESEARCHER: Debra P. Hershkowitz
DESIGN: Debby Jay
DESIGNER: Marjorie Zaum
PRODUCTION COORDINATOR: Joseph Romano

3 5 7 9 8 6 4

Library of Congress Cataloging in Publication Data

Stefoff, Rebecca
  FRIENDSHIP AND LOVE.
  (The Encyclopedia of health)
  Includes index.
  ISBN 0-7910-0039-7
      0-7910-0479-1 (pbk.)
    1. Friendship—Juvenile literature.   2. Intimacy
(Psychology)—Juvenile literature.   3. Love—Juvenile
literature. [1. Friendship.   2. Love.   3. Intimacy
(Psychology)]   I. Title.   II. Series.   88-30032
BF575.F66S73 1988
177'.6

CONTENTS

PREVENTION AND EDUCATION: THE KEYS TO GOOD HEALTH

C. Everett Koop, M.D., Sc.D.
Surgeon General,
U.S. Public Health Service

The issue of health education has received particular attention in recent years because of the presence of AIDS in the news. But our response to this particular tragedy points up a number of broader issues that doctors, public health officials, educators, and the public face. In particular, it points up the necessity for sound health education for citizens of all ages.

Over the past 25 years this country has been able to bring about dramatic declines in the death rates for heart disease, stroke, accidents, and, for people under the age of 45, cancer. Today, Americans generally eat better and take better care of themselves than ever before. Thus, with the help of modern science and technology, they have a better chance of surviving serious—even catastrophic—illnesses. That's the good news.

But, like every phonograph record, there's a flip side, and one with special significance for young adults. According to a report issued in 1979 by Dr. Julius Richmond, my predecessor as Surgeon General, Americans aged 15 to 24 had a higher death rate in 1979 than they did 20 years earlier. The causes: violent death and injury, alcohol and drug abuse, unwanted pregnancies, and sexually transmitted diseases. Adolescents are particularly vulnerable, because they are beginning to explore their own sexuality and perhaps to experiment with drugs. The need for educating young people is critical, and the price of neglect is high.

Yet even for the population as a whole, our health is still far from what it could be. Why? A 1974 Canadian government report attributed all death and disease to four broad elements: inadequacies in the health-care system, behavioral factors or unhealthy life-styles, environmental hazards, and human biological factors.

To be sure, there are diseases that are still beyond the control of even our advanced medical knowledge and techniques. And despite yearnings that are as old as the human race itself, there is no "fountain of youth" to ward off aging and death. Still, there is a solution to many of the problems that undermine sound health. In a word, that solution is prevention. Prevention, which includes health promotion and education, saves lives, improves the quality of life, and, in the long run, saves money.

In the United States, organized public health activities and preventive medicine have a long history. Important milestones include the improvement of sanitary procedures and the development of pasteurized milk in the late 19th century, and the introduction in the mid-20th century of effective vaccines against polio, measles, German measles, mumps, and other once-rampant diseases. Internationally, organized public health efforts began on a wide-scale basis with the International Sanitary Conference of 1851, to which 12 nations sent representatives. The World Health Organization, founded in 1948, continues these efforts under the aegis of the United Nations, with particular emphasis on combatting communicable diseases and the training of health-care workers.

But despite these accomplishments, much remains to be done in the field of prevention. For too long, we have had a medical care system that is science- and technology-based, focused, essentially, on illness and mortality. It is now patently obvious that both the social and the economic costs of such a system are becoming insupportable.

Implementing prevention—and its corollaries, health education and promotion—is the job of several groups of people:

First, the medical and scientific professions need to continue basic scientific research, and here we are making considerable progress. But increased concern with prevention will also have a decided impact on how primary-care doctors practice medicine. With a shift to health-based rather than morbidity-based medicine, the role of the "new physician" will include a healthy dose of patient education.

Second, practitioners of the social and behavioral sciences—psychologists, economists, city planners—along with lawyers, business leaders, and government officials—must solve the practical and ethical dilemmas confronting us: poverty, crime, civil rights, literacy, education, employment, housing, sanitation, environmental protection, health care delivery systems, and so forth. All of these issues affect public health.

Third is the public at large. We'll consider that very important group in a moment.

Fourth, and the linchpin in this effort, is the public health profession—doctors, epidemiologists, teachers—who must harness the professional expertise of the first two groups and the common sense and cooperation of the third, the public. They must define the problems statistically and qualitatively and then help us set priorities for finding the solutions.

To a very large extent, improving those statistics is the responsibility of every individual. So let's consider more specifically what the role of the individual should be and why health education is so important to that role. First, and most obviously, individuals can protect themselves from illness and injury and thus minimize their need for professional medical care. They can eat a nutritious diet, get adequate exercise, avoid tobacco, alcohol, and drugs, and take prudent steps to avoid accidents. The proverbial "apple a day keeps the doctor away" is not so far from the truth, after all.

Second, individuals should actively participate in their own medical care. They should schedule regular medical and dental checkups. Should they develop an illness or injury, they should know when to treat themselves and when to seek professional help. To gain the maximum benefit from any medical treatment that they do require, individuals must become partners in that treatment. For instance, they should understand the effects and side effects of medications. I counsel young physicians that there is no such thing as too much information when talking with patients. But the corollary is the patient must know enough about the nuts and bolts of the healing process to understand what the doctor is telling him. That is at least partially the patient's responsibility.

Education is equally necessary for us to understand the ethical and public policy issues in health care today. Sometimes individuals will encounter these issues in making decisions about their own treatment or that of family members. Other citizens may encounter them as jurors in medical malpractice cases. But we all become involved, indirectly, when we elect our public officials, from school board members to the president. Should surrogate parenting be legal? To what extent is drug testing desirable, legal, or necessary? Should there be public funding for family planning, hospitals, various types of medical research, and medical care for the indigent? How should we allocate scant technological resources, such as kidney dialysis and organ transplants? What is the proper role of government in protecting the rights of patients?

What are the broad goals of public health in the United States today? In 1980, the Public Health Service issued a report aptly entitled *Promoting Health-Preventing Disease: Objectives for the Nation.*This report expressed its goals in terms of mortality and in terms of intermediate goals in education and health improvement. It identified 15 major concerns: controlling high blood pressure; improving family planning; improving pregnancy care and infant health; increasing the rate of immunization; controlling sexually transmitted diseases; controlling the presence of toxic agents and radiation in the environment; improving occupational safety and health; preventing accidents; promoting water fluoridation and dental health; controlling infectious diseases; decreasing smoking; decreasing alcohol and drug abuse; improving nutrition; promoting physical fitness and exercise; and controlling stress and violent behavior.

For healthy adolescents and young adults (ages 15 to 24), the specific goal was a 20% reduction in deaths, with a special focus on motor vehicle injuries and alcohol and drug abuse. For adults (ages 25 to 64), the aim was 25% fewer deaths, with a concentration on heart attacks, strokes, and cancers.

Smoking is perhaps the best example of how individual behavior can have a direct impact on health. Today cigarette smoking is recognized as the most important single preventable cause of death in our society. It is responsible for more cancers and more cancer deaths than any other known agent; is a prime risk factor for heart and blood vessel disease, chronic bronchitis, and emphysema; and is a frequent cause of complications in pregnancies and of babies born prematurely, underweight, or with potentially fatal respiratory and cardiovascular problems.

Since the release of the Surgeon General's first report on smoking in 1964, the proportion of adult smokers has declined substantially, from 43% in 1965 to 30.5% in 1985. Since 1965, 37 million people have quit smoking. Although there is still much work to be done if we are to become a "smoke-free society," it is heartening to note that public health and public education efforts—such as warnings on cigarette packages and bans on broadcast advertising—have already had significant effects.

In 1835, Alexis de Tocqueville, a French visitor to America, wrote, "In America the passion for physical well-being is general." Today, as then, health and fitness are front-page items. But with the greater scientific and technological resources now available to us, we are in a far stronger position to make good health care available to everyone. And with the greater technological threats to us as we approach the 21st century, the need to do so is more urgent than ever before. Comprehensive information about basic biology, preventive medicine, medical and surgical treatments, and related ethical and public policy issues can help you arm yourself with the knowledge you need to be healthy throughout your life.

FOREWORD

Dale C. Garell, M.D.

Advances in our understanding of health and disease during the 20th century have been truly remarkable. Indeed, it could be argued that modern health care is one of the greatest accomplishments in all of human history. In the early 1900s, improvements in sanitation, water treatment, and sewage disposal reduced death rates and increased longevity. Previously untreatable illnesses can now be managed with antibiotics, immunizations, and modern surgical techniques. Discoveries in the fields of immunology, genetic diagnosis, and organ transplantation are revolutionizing the prevention and treatment of disease. Modern medicine is even making inroads against cancer and heart disease, two of the leading causes of death in the United States.

Although there is much to be proud of, medicine continues to face enormous challenges. Science has vanquished diseases such as smallpox and polio, but new killers, most notably AIDS, confront us. Moreover, we now victimize ourselves with what some have called "diseases of choice," or those brought on by drug and alcohol abuse, bad eating habits, and mismanagement of the stresses and strains of contemporary life. The very technology that is doing so much to prolong life has brought with it previously unimaginable ethical dilemmas related to issues of death and dying. The rising cost of health-care is a matter of central concern to us all. And violence in the form of automobile accidents, homicide, and suicide remain the major killers of young adults.

In the past, most people were content to leave health care and medical treatment in the hands of professionals. But since the 1960s, the consumer of medical care—that is, the patient—has assumed an increasingly central role in the management of his or her own health. There has also been a new emphasis placed on prevention: People are recognizing that their own actions can help prevent many of the conditions that have caused death and disease in the past. This accounts for the growing commitment to good nutrition and regular exercise, for the fact that more and more people are choosing not to smoke, and for a new moderation in people's drinking habits.

People want to know more about themselves and their own health. They are curious about their body: its anatomy, physiology, and biochemistry. They want to keep up with rapidly evolving medical technologies and procedures. They are willing to educate themselves about common disorders and diseases so that they can be full partners in their own health-care.

The ENCYCLOPEDIA OF HEALTH is designed to provide the basic knowledge that readers will need if they are to take significant responsibility for their own health. It is also meant to serve as a frame of reference for further study and exploration. The ENCYCLOPEDIA is divided into five subsections: The Healthy Body; The Life Cycle; Medical Disorders & Their Treatment; Psychological Disorders & Their Treatment; and Medical Issues. For each topic covered by the ENCYCLOPEDIA, we present the essential facts about the relevant biology; the symptoms, diagnosis, and treatment of common diseases and disorders; and ways in which you can prevent or reduce the severity of health problems when that is possible. The ENCYCLOPEDIA also projects what may lie ahead in the way of future treatment or prevention strategies.

The broad range of topics and issues covered in the ENCYCLOPEDIA reflects the fact that human health encompasses physical, psychological, social, environmental, and spiritual well-being. Just as the mind and the body are inextricably linked, so, too, is the individual an integral part of the wider world that comprises his or her family, society, and environment. To discuss health in its broadest aspect it is necessary to explore the many ways in which it is connected to such fields as law, social science, public policy, economics, and even religion. And so, the ENCYCLOPEDIA is meant to be a bridge between science, medical technology, the world at large, and you. I hope that it will inspire you to pursue in greater depth particular areas of interest, and that you will take advantage of the suggestions for further reading and the lists of resources and organizations that can provide additional information.

CHAPTER 1

. . . .

THE MANY FACES OF INTIMACY

*So long as we love we serve; so long as we
are loved by others, I might almost say
that we are indispensable; and no man is
useless while he has a friend.*

—*Robert Louis Stevenson,* Across the Plains, *1892*

In all of human history, has any subject occupied more attention, more thought, more imagination than love? It has been
the theme of countless poems, dramas, songs, philosophical spec-
ulations, religious pronouncements, and stories. People of all
eras and all nations have written, sung, or spoken of love. But
what is remarkable about this inexhaustible subject is that it is
forever familiar and yet forever new.

Among the oldest writings known to us are the ancient Egyptian papyri, or scrolls of paper made from the papyrus reed. On
these scrolls, the Egyptians recorded matters of public importance: the births and deaths of kings, records of wars fought and
taxes paid. Yet some of these crumbling papyri also record the
movements of the human heart. One papyrus, written sometime
between 1570 and 1080 B.C.E., or between about 3,500 and 3,000
years ago (B.C.E. stands for Before the Common Era and is equivalent to B.C.), speaks to us across the centuries in words that are
as true to our emotions today as when they were written:

> My love is upon the other side of the river;
> A stretch of water lies between,
> And a crocodile waits upon the sandbank.
> But I go down into the water, I walk upon the flood.

Ruth's devotion to her mother-in-law—described in the Old Testament—remains a profound example of the timeless value of friendship and love.

> Her love comes across the water, turning the waves to
>   solid earth
> For me to walk upon.
> Nothing, nothing can keep me from my love.
> The river is our enchanted sea.

The feelings expressed by this anonymous lover in the ancient world are no different from those that Shakespeare gave to his creations Romeo and Juliet in the 1590s, or those found in any number of Top 40 hit songs we hear on the radio today. Lovers of all eras celebrate their passionate desire to be together and their belief that love can overcome all obstacles. Similarly, rejected lovers grieve and lonely people long for love in the poetry of all times and all places. Love, it seems, is a universal experience.

Friendship, too, has been important to people throughout history and in many cultures. The Bible describes and praises friendship of all kinds, from the devotion of Ruth to her mother-in-law, Naomi, in the Old Testament to the fellowship of the

Apostles in the New Testament. The philosophers of ancient Greece and Rome prized friendship and loyalty highly—perhaps more highly than love, because a friend was regarded as a reflection of one's own virtues and best features. "A friend is, as it were, a second self," said the Roman orator Cicero.

Friendship and love are two aspects of intimacy, which is a shared feeling of closeness between people. Being intimate means different things in different relationships. For example, in the case of two people who love each other but do not necessarily confide in one another or share experiences on a day-to-day basis, such as a teenager and a grandparent, intimacy may take the form of a caring, supportive relationship in which feelings are not often put into words. Between best friends, on the other hand, intimacy may mean hours of conversation and shared confidences or simply the desire to spend time together every day.

In one form or another, intimacy is at the heart of all of our most intense and important relationships—it exists between parents and children, between close friends, between lovers or marriage partners. Only in recent years, however, have we attempted to examine and to understand intimacy in the way that we have tried to understand other types of human activity. Just as philosophers and researchers have used the tools of psychology (the study of mental processes and behavior) and sociology (the study of human social behavior and societies) to explore the learning process and the development of the individual personality, they are now using these tools to explore the nature of intimacy and its role in our lives. They have discovered that intimacy is an essential part of what makes us human. Although cultures and individuals express intimacy in myriad ways, the need for intimacy appears to be universal—and the satisfaction of that need is vitally important.

THE HIERARCHY OF HUMAN NEEDS

Psychologist Abraham Maslow proposed in the 1950s that all human beings share certain needs, which he arranged in a hierarchy, or a series of ranks or levels. In Maslow's thinking, which has been widely accepted by psychologists, people are driven to fulfill all of their needs, but they can strive to fulfill a particular level of need only when all of the levels below it have been fulfilled.

According to Maslow, people have two main sets of needs: basic needs and growth needs. Basic needs are essential to life and must be met before people can fulfill their growth needs. Maslow identified two sets of basic needs and three sets of growth needs, or five levels of human need in all. The hierarchy of needs can best be viewed as a pyramid, with the basic needs on the bottom and the growth needs on the top.

Basic Needs

Physiological Needs The first level of the basic needs—the bottom of the pyramid—consists of physiological needs, or the things our bodies need simply in order to survive: air, food, water, shelter from the elements, and sleep. A person who is deprived of any of these physiological needs will not live long enough to worry about satisfying his higher-level needs.

Safety and Security Once their physiological needs are met, people experience a need for safety and security. This need is partly physical; that is, people need safety from tigers and avalanches, and they need the security of knowing where their next meal is coming from. It is a human characteristic to try to fulfill the need for physical safety and security by some degree of planning for tomorrow: by erecting fences to keep out the tigers, or by planting crops to provide next year's meals.

But emotional safety and security are also necessary if life is to be more than simple survival. People, especially children, who are deprived of feelings of safety and security for long periods of time—prisoners of war, for example, or abused children—may remain alive in body but develop crippling illnesses of the mind and spirit. The development of normal communication skills and memory, the ability to learn, and the formation and maintenance of trust and a stable personality all seem to depend, in part, upon a safe and secure emotional environment.

Growth Needs

Love, Affection, Belonging The first of the growth needs is the need to experience intimacy. Once their basic needs are met, humans need to feel that they are loved. To be loved is not enough, however; people also need to have that love expressed.

The ability to place trust in others appears to depend in part upon having had a secure emotional environment during one's formative years.

In other words, a child's need for love will not be fully met when he is simply told "Of course I love you" by his parent. To satisfy his need, the statement of fact must be accompanied by the symbols of affection: a smile, a warm and loving tone of voice, a hug or kiss. Similarly, men and women are less likely to remain satisfied with love relationships if the expression of affection—through words, through touch, and through shared memories and experiences—is absent.

Another part of the need for intimacy is the need to belong. The individual, personal relationships that satisfy our need for love and affection also allow us to feel that we are important to our loved ones and that we have a place in their lives. On a larger scale, people also hunger for a sense of shared identity or belonging to a community of some sort, whether it be a neighborhood, a group of kids that always eats lunch together at the same table at school, a religion, a sports team, a political movement, or a nation.

Even the child too young to understand endearing words will respond to them if they are spoken warmly and reinforced with physical tenderness.

Esteem and Self-esteem Next in the hierarchy of needs comes the need to feel esteemed by others—that is, to feel respected and valued. Many social and political movements of recent years have recognized this universal human need. The movements to protect the rights and dignity of mentally or physically disabled people and of the homeless are examples, as is the women's movement, which has sought to ensure equal job opportunities and pay for women.

Along with the need to be esteemed by others goes the need to feel self-esteem, or self-respect. This does not mean pride or vanity, although it may take those forms in some cases. Rather, self-esteem means recognition and acceptance of oneself as essentially worthwhile. Maslow placed this level of the hierarchy above the level of love, affection, and belonging because people whose intimacy needs are not met when they are growing up may suffer from low or damaged self-esteem; that is, they may not develop a healthy respect for themselves and their abilities and accomplishments.

Self-actualization The last and highest need, according to Maslow, is self-actualization. People who have fulfilled all of their other needs are free to develop and to act on concepts of truth, justice, beauty, order, humor, and other values. People who achieve this level of fulfillment—and Maslow pointed out that not all of us will do so—are creative, expressive, and at peace with themselves and their lives: a worthwhile goal, surely, and one that cannot be reached without experiencing intimacy along the way.

The Other Half of the Picture

According to Maslow, the need to be loved is part of what makes us human. But the philosopher and psychologist Erich Fromm, writing at about the same time as Maslow, pointed out in a short but important book called *The Art of Loving* that an emphasis on being loved might obscure the other half of the picture. Fromm believed that loving others is at least as important as being loved by others, and that our need to give love is as strong as our need to receive it. True intimacy is not merely the fulfillment of one set of needs; it is a two-way process of giving, taking, and

The Harlem Boys Choir in concert. Most humans prize the pleasure of belonging to a group and sharing in its collective identity.

Andre Viger crosses the finish line of the 90th Boston Marathon in 1986. The physically handicapped have fought for and won the right to be treated with dignity and esteem.

sharing. Fromm expressed the middle level of Maslow's hierarchy not as the need to be loved but as the need for interaction, for a mutual exchange of love and affection.

This need for interaction is a natural, universal desire. Most people experience more than one kind of intimacy in their lives, and it is likely that no one has ever experienced all of the forms that human interaction can take. Relationships, marriages, friendships, family structures, and other intimate interactions vary from culture to culture, from person to person, and even from time to time in an individual's life. Yet all the many forms of intimacy are expressions of the same universal need.

EVERYONE IS AN EXPERT

The hierarchy of human needs shows that the need for intimacy is universal, normal, and even necessary for growth. But the hierarchy gives no descriptions or definitions. It does not tell us anything about the nature of friendship and love. Indeed, the nature of intimacy—what it is, how it works, how to achieve it— remains one of life's great mysteries.

Over the centuries, artists, poets, and writers have described and defined intimacy in hundreds of ways. Scientists and researchers are now adding their contributions: the results of numerous surveys and studies, new terms coined to describe the nuances of feelings and relationships, and helpful tools such as Maslow's hierarchy. But neither poems nor pie charts can tell the whole story of friendship and love.

Despite its universality, intimacy is a deeply individual experience. It enters people's lives and engages their feelings in a multitude of ways. Some psychologists and philosophers have suggested that there may be as many different kinds of love and

Self-actualized people are creative, expressive, and at peace with themselves.

We are all the ultimate authorities on our own experiences of friendship and love.

friendship as there are relationships between or among people; they suggest, in fact, that each experience of intimacy is unique and subtly different from all others. According to this line of thought, the experts—whether passionate poets or serious scientists—can never say all that there is to say about friendship and love. Each of us is the only ultimate authority on our own experiences of friendship or love. Where intimacy is concerned, no one is an expert, and everyone is an expert.

At the same time, the combined wisdom of generations, though it cannot explain everything, is useful. Intimacy and the emotions connected with it can be baffling, confusing, or disturbing. For those of us who are interested in or concerned about this most bewildering and enriching part of life, insights from psychology, history, literature, and anthropology (the study of the differences among human cultures) can offer answers to questions about feelings and relationships, as well as new ways of thinking about friendship and love.

The Name of Love

One of the most perplexing issues connected with intimacy is the problem of naming it. It is easy, for example, to say "friendship and love" and think we know what we mean by each. But it is less easy to give a straightforward definition of each of these simple, everyday words. It is more difficult still to distinguish between them. We love some of our friends, but some of them, perhaps, we only like; and we probably love some people whom we would not describe first and foremost as friends.

What is the difference between an acquaintance and a friend? Between a friend and a best friend? Between liking and loving? Can we love someone we do not like? Do we feel differently toward friends of our own sex than we do toward friends of the opposite sex? At what point can close friendship be called love? What do friendship and love have in common? How do they differ? Can they exist in the same relationship? Most of us believe we can supply answers to at least some of these questions, based on our own history of relationships. But friendship and love can also be the most turbulent and mystifying, as well as the most rewarding, of human activities. This is especially true during adolescence and young adulthood, when old relationships often change and new ones gain importance. The focus shifts from intimacy within the family to relationships with peers and then to romantic and sexual love.

The issue of defining intimacy becomes even more complicated with the addition of sex. Sexual activity is certainly a part of many love relationships and even of some friendships. But, although a loving, intimate relationship may be considered the ideal context for sex, sexual activity can take place quite independently of love and friendship. Sexual attraction usually plays some part in the process we call "falling in love." But the various stages of sexual passion do not exactly coincide with those of a long-term, intimate love relationship. In some cases, in fact, our sexual desire for an attractive person conflicts with our emotional desire to preserve and protect an intimate relationship with someone else we love. Friendship, love, and sex are sometimes in harmony and sometimes in conflict. But the more we know about human intimacy in general, the greater is our ability to increase the harmony and decrease the conflict in our own relationships.

Psychologists, historians, and anthropologists have assembled vocabularies to discriminate among feelings, relationships, and types of behavior. Some of the terms they use are found in the following chapters. Actually, there are many kinds and degrees of friendship, love, and sexual passion, and these three aspects of intimacy can be interconnected in many ways. No single category of intimacy is watertight; each term we use to describe our intimate relationships overlaps with one or two other terms, just as each relationship has various shadings and nuances.

      •   •   •   •

CHAPTER 2

HOW WE LEARN TO LOVE

Give a little love to a child, and you get a great deal back.

—*John Ruskin,* The Crown of Wild Olive, *1866*

In recent decades, many psychologists and social scientists have come to believe that human life can best be understood as a continuous, ongoing process of development on several simultaneous levels. One such level that is apparent to everyone is the level of physiological, or bodily, development. People are born physically small and immature; as they grow, they develop into physiological adulthood. Each of the various stages of growth—infancy, childhood, puberty, adolescence, adulthood, and old age—is associated with certain physiological characteristics and processes, such as the appearance of teeth in early childhood, the "growth spurt" of puberty, or the slowing of reflexes that usually accompanies old age.

Because this process of physiological development is universal and very visible, it seems natural to think of our lives in terms of these stages and to group other people together by general age groups, or developmental stages of physiological growth. For example, one of the first two things you are likely to mention when describing another person is his or her general age group: "kid," "teenager," "adult," "old man," or the like. (The other is his or her gender.) Unlike age, however, other developmental processes are not so easily identified.

Just as individuals develop physically, they also develop psychologically and socially. Psychological development is internal, rather than external. It is concerned with the growth of what psychologists call the intellectual and affective capacities. Intellectual capacity, or mental development, refers to the ability to perform certain kinds of thought processes; affective capacity, or emotional development, refers to the ability to experience and express feelings. Social development, which parallels external physiological and internal psychological development, refers to an individual's ability to interact with other people in ways that are successful—that is, in ways that are satisfactory to that individual. The experiences of friendship and love involve both our emotional development, or feelings, and our social development, or interactions with others.

These three processes of development—physiological, psychological, and social—occur in everyone, but everyone does not proceed through them at the same rate. Some young people shoot up in height between the ages of 12 and 14, growing 4 inches or more in less than a year; others achieve their full height at a slower rate or later in their teen years. Similarly, some young adults may become interested in the opposite sex and in dating while their classmates of the same age remain more interested

Some young adults develop an interest in dating before their peers do.

in sports, games, and hanging out with their friends. Not only do rates of development differ from person to person, but most individuals develop at different rates on different levels. It is not at all uncommon, for example, for a young child to seem "grown-up" for his age because of advanced intellectual or social skills, or for a teenager who gets good grades and shows other evidence of high-level intellectual capacities to feel awkward and immature on a first date or in some other social situation.

THREE MODELS OF DEVELOPMENT

Psychologists and social scientists have devised a number of developmental models, or theories about stages of development. No single developmental model is universally accepted as the sole explanation of individual development, but each of the following three influential and widely accepted models offers a perspective for examining friendship, love, and sexuality and their place in human life.

Freud's Model

Sigmund Freud (1856–1939), a Viennese psychiatrist and psychoanalyst, developed many theories about the structure and operation of the mind. Believing that the mental health or disorder of the individual is caused by events, family relationships, and sexual feelings in very early childhood, Freud paid particular attention to the ways in which children develop.

He concluded that individual development comes about through the interplay of two powerful forces that he called the pleasure principle and the reality principle. According to Freud's pleasure principle, humans are born with an instinctive desire to seek pleasure. For an infant, pleasure may be food, warmth, or being held; for an older person, it may be sex, money, power, or creative satisfaction. Infants and small children expect their desires for pleasure to be satisfied immediately; for example, a baby who is screaming for food or attention will not be soothed by a mother who says, "Just a minute, dear," from across the room. But as children grow older, the pleasure principle comes into conflict with the reality principle. In other words, children and adolescents gradually learn that the world is not organized in such a

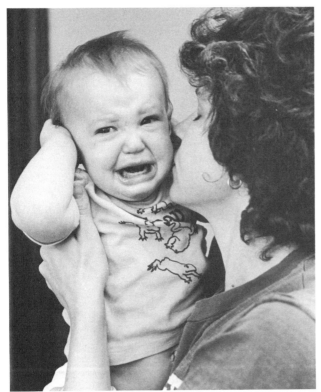

Every infant expects to be held and comforted as soon as he cries. Sigmund Freud equated this expectation with the "pleasure principle"— the belief, formed early in childhood, that all desires deserve instant gratification.

way as to grant immediate and total satisfaction of their desires for pleasure. They learn to wait until mealtime when they are hungry, to take turns playing with toys, and to save money for desired purchases. These are some of the realities of life.

Children growing up also learn that other people—parents, brothers and sisters, teachers, and friends—have independent desires and lives of their own. To a baby, a mother is like a part of himself that exists to provide the food, comfort, and attention that the baby craves. As the baby gets older, he realizes that his mother is a separate person who will not always be able to satisfy all of his needs. In fact, he sees that his mother and other people have needs of their own that he may be expected to meet. This, too, is part of reality. Friendship and love can be viewed as attempts to recapture or prolong the early state in which other people are sources of pleasure. Successful friendships and love relationships achieve a working balance of the pleasure and reality principles.

Today, many psychologists and philosophers think that Freud's view of human nature and development is too narrow and limited to account for the complexity of human emotions and relationships and for the many forms of friendship and love. Freud believed that people are driven by instincts, or inborn urges and patterns over which they have little or no conscious power. But more recent theorists tend to give less weight to instinct and more weight to the conscious choices of individuals in shaping their own development. In addition, Freud's belief that all human desires, activities, and relationships are rooted in sexual drives and feelings is no longer widely accepted.

Piaget's Model

Jean Piaget (1896–1980), a Swiss psychologist, studied the intellectual development of children—how and when they acquire certain types of understanding, such as knowing what the concept of "tomorrow" means or being able to solve problems. He divided childhood and adolescence into four stages, each with its own way of looking at the world.

Sensorimotor Stage The term *sensorimotor* refers to the five senses and to motion. During this stage, which lasts for about the first two years of life, the child is preoccupied with sights, sounds, and other sense impressions, and also with mastering his motor skills, such as the ability to pick things up, to stand, and to walk.

Preoperational Stage The preoperational stage lasts from about age two to age six or seven. During this stage, the child learns to use words as symbols for things in the world around him. He begins to interact with other people through language.

Concrete-Operational Stage Around age seven, the child enters the concrete-operational stage, which lasts for four or five years. During this stage, he begins to understand abstract concepts such as time and distance, and he also begins to be able to think logically, in a systematic, problem-solving manner.

Operational Stage The final stage begins at around age 12 and lasts for the rest of the individual's lifetime. This "fully developed" adult thinking features reasoning, logic, and problem solving.

Although Piaget was primarily interested in development on the intellectual level, he noted that the various levels of devel-

During the sensorimotor stage of development—described by Jean Piaget—the child is preoccupied with mastering motor skills.

opment are interconnected. The child's emotions, body, and social skills—things that help shape his friendships and love relationships—grow and develop along with his mental abilities.

During the sensorimotor stage, for example, the infant smiles at familiar people, shows uneasiness or distress around strangers, and becomes anxious when he is separated from his mother (or whoever is his primary caretaker). In the next stage of mental development, the child begins to name his feelings. He also absorbs approval or disapproval, in the form of statements such as "Big boys don't cry," and "Maybe Tommy will share his toys if you ask him nicely," of his feelings and social behavior. His growing language skill allows him to interact with more people, and this in turn helps his emotions to mature and improves his social skills. As he approaches adolescence, his more sophisticated language abilities and mental skills enable him to become increasingly independent of his family. His world expands to include friends, age-group peers, schoolmates, and eventually romantic partners. He also becomes capable of forming the abstract values—honesty, intelligence, popularity, beauty, or any combination of qualities—that guide him toward certain people and relationships and away from others.

Erikson's Model

Both Freud's and Piaget's developmental models assume that the child grows from infancy toward a final, adult, or "finished," point. But psychologist Erik Erikson (b. 1902) took a different approach. In Erikson's model, development is not limited to childhood and adolescence. It is a never-ending, lifelong process, with eight stages. Each stage can be viewed as a conflict between two opposing forces; one force promotes healthy mental, emotional, and social growth, whereas the other stunts growth.

Stage 1: Trust versus mistrust. In infancy, the baby who is cared for and loved will develop trust in others and a sense of his own identity. Healthy development in this first stage is the basis for a trusting, open attitude toward later intimate relationships.

Piaget theorized that each child's social skills and his ability to form friendships develop gradually as his mental abilites grow.

Stage 2: Autonomy versus shame and doubt. In this stage, toddlers in supportive, caring environments develop healthy self-esteem and self-confidence. They are made to feel capable and worthy, whereas those not so fortunate will develop doubts about their lovability.

Stage 3: Initiative versus guilt. Later, small children begin to develop awareness of their sexual identities; that is, they identify with boys or girls, men or women. They also discover the power of learning. In a healthy environment, curiosity and the beginnings of independence are praised or encouraged. Those whose first stirrings of independence, curiosity, or sexual identity are punished will feel a burden of guilt.

Stage 4: Industry versus inferiority. As they grow older, children continue to develop sexual identities. They also discover the connection between work (studying or chores) and results (good grades or allowance money), and they begin to make value judgments about other people. Children whose efforts are praised and guided in this stage will develop productive values, whereas those whose efforts are ignored or ridiculed will develop feelings of profound inferiority.

Stage 5: Identity versus role confusion. This is the stage of puberty and adolescence, when teenagers begin to create identities for themselves outside their families through cliques (small groups of friends with the same interests), close friends, and love relationships. They also begin to grapple with another form of identity: the role or occupation they will fill in life.

Stage 6: Intimacy versus isolation. As the young adult brings his or her newly established identity into the world of intimate relationships (including sexual ones), he or she strives to form bonds of commitment and sharing.

Stage 7: Generativity versus stagnation. At this point, healthy mature adults express themselves through some form of creative or productive activity, such as rewarding work, happy relationships, a place in the community, learning or teaching, or raising a family. Erikson called this self-expression generativity, meaning "giving or creating something new." The opposite state, stagnation, refers to a passive or unfulfilling way of life in which the individual feels that he contributes nothing to the world.

Stage 8: Ego integrity versus despair. In late maturity and old age, the seven earlier stages ripen into a healthy form of self-

According to Erik Erikson, rewarding work, such as teaching, gives mature adults a means of personal expression.

satisfaction. A person who feels that he or she has done a good job of taking care of the business of the earlier stages will be able to face and accept approaching death with feelings of accomplishment and inner peace. Erikson called this state ego integrity. Freud defined the ego as the personality or sense of self that includes identity, potential, and achievement. Ego integrity means satisfaction with oneself and one's life; its opposite, despair, is dissatisfaction or feelings of failure in life, love, or work.

These three models and many others offer different perspectives on personality development. But they have one important thing in common: All of them emphasize the importance of infancy and childhood, during which the foundations of emotional and social development—and of all intimate relationships—are laid. It is during these years, in fact, that we learn to love.

THE ROOTS OF LOVE

The relationship between parents and children—especially that between the mother, who for thousands of years of human history was the primary child rearer, and her offspring—has often been described as the highest, most unselfish, kind of love. Today, psychologists recognize that the relationship between a mother (or father, other relative, or primary caretaker) and an infant is a vitally important element in the infant's development, as well as an expression of powerful feelings of caring on the part of the mother. The mother-child relationship can be viewed as the child's preparation for friendship and love, for to a greater or lesser degree it will shape all other relationships in his life.

Attachment and Intimacy

The infant's connection with his mother is sometimes called attachment by psychologists to distinguish it from the more conscious kind of love that the child usually develops for his parents a few years later. Attachment is almost instinctive. It refers to the child's dependency on the mother, a dependency that can be explained in terms of Maslow's hierarchy of needs. A human infant is too weak and undeveloped to survive without a caretaker; therefore, the infant depends upon his mother to meet his basic needs, first for food and warmth and then for safety and security. Once these needs are met, the infant experiences a need for love, affection, and a sense of belonging. Although the child may be surrounded by loving people, the mother remains the primary satisfier of these needs as well.

From as early as a few weeks after birth, babies show that they recognize their mothers (or primary caretakers). Because the babies' needs are satisfied when they are with their mothers, they develop strong feelings of attachment to their mothers and feel discomfort, anxiety, and distress when they are separated from them. For this reason, babies and small children often cry when they are held by strangers or turned over to baby-sitters for the first time. But a baby whose mother is consistently affectionate and reassuring gradually learns that the attachment can survive brief periods of separation—the mother will return and the infant's needs will once again be met. By age three or four, the anxiety of separation has begun to diminish. By this age, also, the child is better prepared to tolerate a separation from his mother because he has new sources of pleasure—toys, games, and other people. He has learned that he can enjoy these pleasures without needing his mother's presence every minute.

Although it is slowly outgrown, the early attachment of the infant to the mother is, for most people, the first experience of emotional attachment to another person. If the mother-child relationship is stable, warm, and loving, the child will approach other relationships with trust, self-confidence, and affection. If, however, the mother-child relationship is lacking in warmth or security, as is sadly sometimes the case, the child may develop feelings of hostility, confusion, anger, or lack of trust toward other people that will make it difficult for him to have successful friendships or love relationships.

A number of social science research studies (beginning with the two-decade-long study conducted by British psychologist John Bowlby, who followed the progress of children separated from their parents during World War II) have shown that children who do not experience warm, affectionate, supportive attachments have a greater than normal chance of encountering certain problems later in life. These problems include poor grades, de-

A secure and loving attachment with our parents is the foundation for a lifetime of intimacy with others.

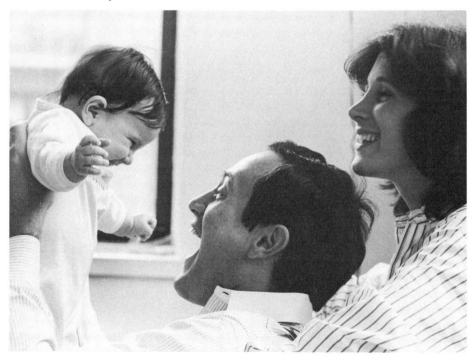

linquency or trouble with the law, alcoholism or drug abuse, failure to establish intimate relationships, divorce, depression, and even suicide. Naturally, results such as those found in these studies do not mean that every child whose relationship with his or her parents is not perfect will encounter these problems— most will not. It merely means that many of the people who do experience problems in life also report poor or unsatisfactory early attachments, childhoods spent in one or more foster homes (homes other than those of the children's parents, where the children may be placed by social services), or histories of child abuse. Fortunately, such unhappy instances are the exception, rather than the norm, and their harmful effects can often be countered with counseling and therapy. On the other hand, psychologists believe, a secure and loving attachment between an infant and its mother or parents—the kind of attachment that most often exists—is the best possible foundation for a lifetime of intimacy. The attachment to its mother teaches the infant two important lessons: that one is worthy of being loved and that it is safe and pleasurable to depend upon and love others.

●　　　●　　　●　　　●

CHAPTER 3

· · · · · · · · · · · · ·

OUR FIRST FRIENDSHIPS

Each friend represents a world in us,
a world possibly not born until they arrive,
and it is only by this meeting
that a new world is born.

—*Anaïs Nin,* The Diary of Anaïs Nin, Vol. II, *1937*

In order for a small child to mature, the intense attachment that he feels for his mother must fade. It is an attachment born of dependency, and as the child grows older he inevitably becomes less and less dependent—or, to look at it another way, more and more independent. He undergoes a process that psychologists refer to as individuation. That is, he comes to be aware of himself as an individual being, apart from his mother, and as time passes he takes more and more responsibility for himself.

The fading of the infant's attachment should not be regarded as a loss, or as a lessening of love. What happens is that, as the infant becomes an individual in his own right, his response to his mother and others around him is no longer governed by his natural craving for protection, comfort, and security. Instead, he becomes capable of progressively richer interactions with others. His affection for his mother and other loved ones takes on a quality of awareness, choice, and communication rather than instinct. Interaction becomes a two-way affair, in which the child receives love and responds by returning it.

The baby's universe at first consists of one relationship, with the mother (or primary caretaker). Soon, however, the child begins to recognize and interact with other inhabitants of that universe. These may include the father, brothers and sisters, grandparents, family friends, or anyone who is a familiar and

The first people an infant learns to interact with—aside from his parents—are other family members, especially siblings.

affectionate presence. At this point, the child has made an immense leap of the heart—he has taken the feelings of attachment he once felt for his mother alone and begun to transfer them to other people. He has entered the familial phase of his emotional development.

Throughout the years of childhood, up to about the age of 9 or 10, the family is the child's world. More than a day-care center, nursery school, or school, the family is the source of the child's values and sense of identity. Each family is a network of personalities, customs, habits, routines, and beliefs that surrounds, supports, and shapes its individual members. Whether we adopt their values or rebel against them, we all react to our families in some way. And many psychologists believe that our later experiences of love and friendship are reflections of our early family relationships. For example, a girl who has a happy and loving relationship with her father might later fall in love with and marry a man who possesses the good qualities that she admired and respected in her father. On the other hand, a girl whose father seems cold, distant, and difficult to please might later choose a husband with the opposite qualities. Or, she might choose a mate with the same negative qualities because she is still driven to seek approval and love from her father or someone like him. Frequently, these sorts of choices are made with no conscious awareness of motive.

After the child has established himself as an individual within his family, he must begin another psychological process called separation. This is the process by which the child gradually separates from his family in preparation for his own adult life of work, love, and perhaps another family. The child's relationships of love and intimacy with his family do not end, of course, but they do change—and change is an inevitable part of the healthy, normal process of growing up. The first big change occurs when the child discovers friendship.

Childhood Friendships

Small children quickly become accustomed to being around peers (others like themselves—in this case, children outside the family). Those who have brothers and sisters may find it a little easier to get used to interacting with peers because they have had practice in playing, sharing, and maybe even fighting with other children. Some psychologists believe that only children may experience difficulty sharing and feeling equal to other children because they have not been brought up with siblings. Other psychologists believe that only children, having spent more time with adults, are often able to demonstrate social and language skills that are advanced for their ages, and these skills can also help them get along with their peers.

Children's relationships with peers pass through several stages. Children up to the age of 4 or 5 usually prefer playing together to playing in isolation, but social scientists who have studied their patterns of play have found that, even when playing side

Children under 5 years old like the company of others their own age but often prefer to play alongside, rather than with, them.

by side, the children spend most of the time talking to themselves and making up games and "rules" for themselves. They coexist, but they do not often collaborate. And feelings of attachment to each other, although intense, are somewhat superficial by adult standards. One study of preschool children in a day-care center showed that children of that age are quite likely to say to each other, "You're my best friend" on Monday and then, on Tuesday, say, "You're not my friend today." Few of the long-enduring friendships of our lives are formed in our preschool years; those that appear to be are most likely actually based on years of interaction later on.

Small children tend to regard any playmate as a friend—the child who shares a sandbox for an hour as well as the child who lives next door. Preschool children seldom talk about their playmates when they are home with their families; in fact, parents are sometimes puzzled when their children do not seem to remember the names of the boys or girls they played with all day. The friendships of small children, in other words, exist in the moment and are based primarily on physical togetherness. These early friendships, however, are of great importance, for they teach skills of cooperation, sharing, self-assertion, and communication that children will carry with them into the next stage of friendship.

As children progress through elementary school, they gain greater familiarity with their peer group. When they become old enough to go outside the house, to the playground, or to school by themselves they begin to seek out each other's company. And they develop the ideas of individual personality characteristics and continuing interaction that we generally associate with friendship. That is, a 4-year-old might say, "Jamie is my friend because Jamie plays with me," but a 9-year-old child might say, "Jamie is my friend because I like him."

The Imaginary Friend Everyone wants to have friends. Most children, however, go through periods of uncertainty about their ability to form friendships. This is why so many children have "imaginary friends." The imaginary friend may be a childhood toy, such as a stuffed animal, which the child names and insists is alive, or it may be a somewhat older child's invisible playmate, confidant, or made-up sibling. It is not uncommon for a child to develop a very elaborate relationship with his or her imaginary friend. Children of preschool age often prattle to these "friends" as they play, and children as old as their early teens may talk to them in private, carry on mental conversations with them, or write letters to them.

Some parents worry that their children are devoting too much time and energy to these imaginary friendships, or that the friendships are unhealthy or abnormal. But psychologists say that they are quite normal; they may become a problem only if they continue into a child's teenage years and keep him or her from building real-life friendships, or if they cause bizarre behavior. For the most part, imaginary friendships boost children's self-esteem, express their playfulness and imaginative creativity, and offer a chance to experiment with friendship without the risk of rejection. They are practice for the other kinds of friendship that await.

The Best Friend The period from about age 9 to age 12 is sometimes called *preadolescence*. By this age, children are deeply involved in the slow, years-long process of separation, or preparing for life outside their families. As a result, friendships and relationships with peers are extremely important to preadolescent children. At this point, children start showing their inde-

Imaginary friendships enable many children to experiment with friendships but also spare them the risk of being rejected.

41

pendence from their families by getting wrapped up in the world of their friends. Preadolescents sometimes feel confused, or as though they were being pulled in two directions at once. An example of this is when they suddenly feel that they would rather do something with their friends than with their parents, or when they start worrying about what their friends will think of their parents. This pull into the outside world is sometimes difficult for children—and their parents—to accept, yet it is natural and necessary.

Most preadolescents have "best friends," people to whom they feel especially close and who return the feeling. Many things can make a best friend: shared interests or hobbies, a history of knowing each other from nursery school on, or even an "alliance" of two people who feel unpopular. But best friendships generally have certain things in common, such as the ability to tell and keep secrets, the responsibility of helping and standing up for each other, and the feeling that best friends know each other better than anyone else.

In short, a best friendship is a form of true intimacy, and it is usually the first experience we have of intimacy outside our families. It allows us to experience the exhilaration of being chosen in a way that our families, however loving, cannot give us. We are born into our families, but we earn our friendships—and being someone's friend makes us feel good about ourselves. This feeling of self-esteem is one of the rewards of intimacy, as we learn when we begin to form friendships. Our relationships with our first close friends also teach us about the excitements, con-

Most preadolescents have a best friend—someone with whom they share secrets, interests, and the feeling that each knows the other better than anyone else.

Many adolescents come to terms with their sexual identity by belonging to a single-gender group.

fidences, fights, reunions, discoveries and self-discoveries, disappointments, losses, and triumphs of intimate relationships. They teach us the give-and-take that is needed to make a friendship work.

Although most best friendships—especially those formed early in life—do not last forever, each feels at the time as though it will. But friendships usually change as the people in them change, and change occurs rapidly during the preadolescent years. This means that preadolescent friendships are likely to change rapidly, as individual interests, tastes, habits, and values change.

Nearly everyone has had the experience of losing a close friend, either through a fight or through a gradual drifting apart. These losses are painful, and sometimes they cause us to wonder whether we are capable of having friends. Yet even short-lived friendships enrich our lives with fun, intimacy, good memories, and experiences that we can draw on for our next friendship.

The Group Another form of friendship that becomes important to children in the preadolescent years is belonging to a group. Social scientists have concluded that humans are by nature gregarious—that is, they tend to form groups, rather than going about the business of life as solitary individuals. During the preadolescent years, when they have matured enough so that they do not have to be tended by a parent at all times, most children begin to attach themselves to groups of friends or playmates.

A 10-year-old usually will identify children in his class at school as either part of his group of friends or not. A group may contain one or more pairs of best friends, but all members of the group consider each other friends to some degree. Frequently children who think of themselves as a group will refuse to allow other children to play with them; they guard the boundaries of their group jealously. But the membership of the group can change very quickly, so that someone who was "outside" yesterday may be "inside" today.

One interesting feature of friendship groups among preadolescents is that they are almost always all-boy or all-girl groups. Preschoolers and children in elementary school do not show much awareness of sex differences and are likely to form "sandbox friendships" with children of both sexes. But by preadolescence, that has changed. One study, conducted from 1975 to 1978 by psychologist Janet Ward Schofield at a school in Connecticut, revealed that groups of children who ate lunch and walked to and from school together were made up of all boys or all girls more than 95% of the time. Nearly all of the children who were interviewed said that they expected to marry someone of the opposite sex when they grow up—they just did not want to hang around with them right now.

Preadolescents are confronted with a massive task, the challenge of creating their own identities in the world outside the family. They need reassurance of their worthiness, lovability, and popularity from their peers, rather than just from their relatives. As part of the process of individuation and separation, the preadolescent must confirm his or her sexual identity. One way that young people do this is by banding together with others of the same sex. Another way is by setting themselves in opposition to the other sex. For this reason, interaction between the sexes during the preadolescent years is often characterized by teasing, insults, and announcements by boys that they do not want anything to do with girls and statements by girls that boys are stupid.

This behavior is more pronounced in groups than in individuals. For example, an 11-year-old boy may have a neighborhood friend who is a girl and with whom he enjoys talking or watching television, but he will not include her in activities with his group of male friends. This temporary social separation by sex—even occasional hostility toward the opposite sex—seems to be a natural and fairly universal part of growing up. But in the next stage of development, disdain for the opposite sex will turn into consuming interest, as adolescents continue the process of individuation and discover the possibilities of romantic love.

CHAPTER 4

. . . .

ADOLESCENCE AND ADULTHOOD

One word
Frees us from all the weight and pain of life:
That word is love.

—*Sophocles,* Oedipus at Colonus, *406 B.C.E.*

Peer relationships continue to gain importance as preadolescents become teenagers. A great widening of the world occurs during the teen years, or period of adolescence. The process of separation from the family picks up speed, and adolescents quite often begin to give more weight to the opinions of their peers than to those of their parents. Most teenage girls, for example, are far more likely to seek their friends' rather than their parents' approval of their hairstyles and clothing. Parents are sometimes hurt by or resentful of the growing importance of peer relationships, which can seem to threaten their own connection with their child. In fact, arguments between teenagers and parents often occur when the values of the peer group conflict with the parents' values rather than reinforce them.

Adolescence is a time of overlap between the roles of childhood and adulthood. At times, neither role quite fits, and even the most well-balanced teenager will experience some stress and anxiety. During this time, many young people find that their intimacy with their parents is somewhat strained. In addition, they are beginning to think about the possibilities and responsibilities of their futures. For these reasons, friendship is both a central source of emotional support and well-being and an arena in which to practice and test social skills. The social world of the teenager is vastly more complex than that of the child.

Family relations can grow strained when teens feel torn between their parents' values and those of their peer group.

JOINERS AND LONERS

Belonging to a group is even more important to a teenager than to a preadolescent. Teenagers feel the pressure to complete the process of separating themselves from their families, yet they also feel a deep need for some form of affiliation, or group membership, to replace the closeness and security that they used to feel in the family bond. It is for this reason that many teenagers place such emphasis on cliques, popularity, and being part of the "right" group. Everyone wants to feel needed and accepted.

It is easy to see the advantages of being accepted by a close-knit group, or clique, of friends. Being part of a group eases the feelings of loneliness that many adolescents experience as their relationships with family members undergo inevitable changes. A group is a source of identity; it helps define its members, and some of its qualities rub off onto them. If, for example, you are a member of a group that is recognized as jocks, or troublemakers, or straight-A students, that says something about you to the world. And if, within your group, you have a recognized role—

leader, joker, brain, or whatever—that also gives you an identity.

A group can bolster the self-esteem of someone who feels insecure and can give its members the chance to learn the skills of leadership, compromise, and communication. But the intense and complex group friendships of teenagers have a negative side as well. Sometimes the identity that is given to an individual by a group or by his role in the group keeps him from growing. For example, a young man whose self-image centers around his popularity with his school's athletes may not allow the part of himself that enjoys drawing and painting to develop. And cliques can be extremely hurtful to those who are rejected or excluded. Often those who cannot gain membership in the most popular cliques or groups combine to form their own groups.

There are very few true loners among teenagers. Most adolescents, including those who identify with the popular media image of the isolated rebel, feel a strong need to have some kind of interaction with their peers—even if their peers all think of themselves as loners, too. Some adolescents have difficulty navigating the tricky waters of teenage social life; their friendships always seem to run aground, or they feel as though they are adrift in a lifeboat with no help in sight. For those whose interactions are

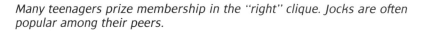

Many teenagers prize membership in the "right" clique. Jocks are often popular among their peers.

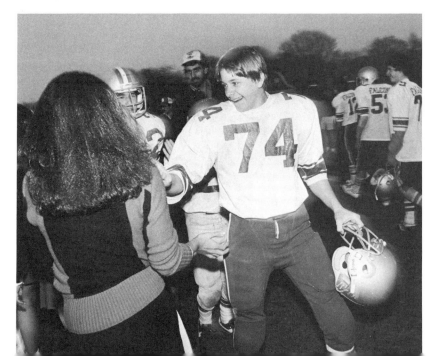

consistently unsatisfactory or unsuccessful, a school nurse, member of the clergy, family doctor, or neighborhood health clinic should be able to recommend some helpful reading or counseling.

PUBERTY AND ROMANCE

The uncertainties and social complexities of adolescence are further complicated by puberty, a period of approximately two years during which the body's reproductive system becomes physically mature. Puberty usually occurs at around age 12 or 13 in girls and age 13 or 14 in boys, although there is a great deal of individual variation in the age at which it begins and the rate at which it progresses.

During puberty, which marks the beginning of adolescence, the bodies of both boys and girls produce large amounts of hormones, chemical substances that accelerate the development of the sexual organs and the appearance of sexual characteristics. Girls develop larger breasts and begin to menstruate, a sign that they will soon be able to bear children. Boys' voices become deeper, their whiskers appear, and their height usually increases by several inches. But the sudden surge of hormones produces more than just physical changes. Along with reproductive maturity come new sexual feelings joined by an interest in the opposite sex.

These new feelings and desires are not always welcome. Many adolescents, in fact, feel confused or fearful about the physical changes that are taking place in their body and the other changes that are taking place in their thoughts and emotions. In addition, hormones produced by the body's glands during adolescence can affect one's feelings. Often they magnify all emotions and mood swings, so that a teenager's typical day can easily include a fit of anger at his parents, a great time laughing with friends, and a solitary crying spell. This emotional excitability makes it even harder to sort out and talk about sexual issues.

One thing that happens during puberty is that the wall that preadolescents build between themselves and the opposite sex begins to break down. After a few years of scorn for boys, girls now want to attract their attention. In fact, girls usually reach this point a year or two before boys; this is why it is sometimes said that girls "mature more quickly" than boys. For a year or so, until the sexual maturity of boys their own age catches up with them, girls are likely to be interested in boys who are slightly older than themselves.

Sooner or later, however, adolescents enter the exciting and sometimes intimidating world of romance. For many, their introduction into this new world is a lot like the imaginary friendships of their much younger years—it takes the form of a crush. Having a crush (an intense, one-sided infatuation that is usually not acted on) is a way of getting used to feelings of attraction and sexual excitement, of imagining yourself in a relationship, of testing the emotional waters before plunging in. Boys and girls alike have crushes. Their first crushes are often on people such as rock singers, actors and actresses, or fashion models, who are entirely outside adolescents' everyday lives. These intense crushes are perfectly normal; in fact, they are almost universal in modern Western society, and sometimes, in the form of occasional fantasies or daydreams, they continue to occupy a special place in our thoughts even after we have begun to experience real-life relationships of our own.

These crushes on distant, out-of-reach people are attractive during early adolescence precisely because the people to whom they are directed are unattainable. In the early stages of sexual interest, many preteens and teenagers feel safer directing their energies toward someone who will not threaten them with a response. With time and increasing confidence, however, they direct their attentions to people who are closer to home, although possibly still out of reach: a teacher, perhaps, or an older boy or girl who is not at all interested in a young admirer. Again, this is a normal part of emotional development. It causes difficulties only in those rare cases when the adolescent loses sight of reality and expects a response that is inappropriate. In most cases, though, the attraction that teenagers feel toward distant, out-of-reach figures is soon transferred to other teenagers with whom they can interact.

Falling in Love

During the teenage years, most people have their first experience of what is called "falling in love." This is a state of intense attraction to another person, together with a seemingly irresistible desire to be with that person and a delight in shared feelings and

Most people first "fall in love" during their teenage years.

experiences. The initial phase of falling in love—in which the attraction seems overwhelming and the loved one appears to be perfect—is sometimes called infatuation, although that term generally suggests an attraction that is superficial and will fade, rather than one that is deep and will endure.

Psychologist Dorothy Tennov has invented another word to describe the state of falling in love. She calls it limerence, and she uses it to refer to the exciting time at the beginning of a new relationship when the attraction is strong and the partners are in the process of discovering one another. Limerence is a powerful, almost intoxicating feeling, but it is not the same thing as love, which Tennov defines as a longer-lasting relationship between people who know each other well and make a commitment to one another. To put it another way, limerence is the process of falling in love, whereas love itself is the state of being in love over time. Limerence can turn into love, but not all limerent relationships will become love relationships.

One question that nearly all adolescents ask at some time is: Is this love? Often a teenager believes that he or she is deeply in love, only to grow angry and frustrated when parents and others dismiss the relationship as a childish crush or an infatuation. Often, too, teenagers themselves are unsure of their feelings— and this is only natural, as these feelings are not only new, but changeable and highly individual. After all, if the poets and scientists of the past 4,000 years have been unable to agree on a definition of love, why should a 14 year old be sure of it?

Feelings of romance and sexuality during adolescence take many different forms, from crushes on movie stars to falling in love for the first time. In addition, teenagers become involved in romances for many reasons, some of which have little to do with the actual relationship—to keep in step with friends who are dating, for example, or to assert independence from their parents. Teenagers who recognize that they can experience strong feelings of love and desire for someone without necessarily expecting to be in love with that person forever have a good chance of weathering the emotional storms of adolescence and getting their feelings sorted out.

Adolescence is a time of experimentation. As we move into the world outside our families, we have the ability to meet and get to know many different kinds of people, to discover what we like and what we do not like in others. Love relationships in adolescence—and friendships, too—are an important part of this process. But although the thrills and hurts of each relationship are just as real and vivid as those experienced by older people, they generally do not last as long. The fast-changing, up-and-down nature of teenage romances does not diminish their intensity; it only means that few of them will outlast adolescence. By the end of adolescence, however, the period of separation and testing the waters is ending for most people, and the search begins for an enduring relationship.

Maturity

Puberty brings with it sexual, or reproductive, maturity. But to say that adolescents are physically capable of becoming fathers and mothers is not to say that they are ready to do so. Unlike animals, whose lives are directed by instinct and who begin to breed as soon as they reach reproductive maturity, human beings require many years of care before they can survive on their own. They live in a social world that is directed by a vast body of knowledge, custom, and experience that must be passed from parents to children.

Survival in the human world requires education, preparation, and training. Unlike animals, most of us are not going to live in the woods and catch our food. We need homes and jobs. To attain these things, or to provide them for our loved ones, requires that we function effectively in the human world. And in order to do that, we must reach emotional and social maturity as well as physical maturity. Our emotional and social selves, however, do not develop as rapidly as our bodies.

In a sense, nature plays a cruel joke on humans, because our bodies are ready for sexual adulthood long before our minds and feelings are. One of the most difficult challenges facing teenagers, especially in modern Western societies, where the two sexes mingle at school and are permitted to date, is to make responsible decisions about sexual behavior and to act in ways that will enhance, not hinder, their own social and emotional growth and that of others.

Adult Intimacy

The process of growing up can be seen as a gradual moving outward, from the intense one-to-one relationship of the infant and its mother, to the progressively wider worlds of family, peers, friends of the same sex, and finally the complex adolescent world of friendship and love. During this progression, the individual is establishing an independent identity. Adolescence is the final, crucial phase of this movement toward independence; that is why the teenage years are often stormy ones, full of rebellion and testing the bonds of family love. At the time, adolescents and their parents sometimes overlook the fact that, although their relationships may be changing, they are still important. As we progress to new levels, we do not leave the older levels behind— we build on them. But, in the normal course of things, we cannot return to an earlier level of existence. A child cannot go back to depending upon his mother as an infant does, and an adolescent cannot retreat into a protective haven of family relationships and turn his back on the beckoning world.

There is a degree of irony in the process of growing up and separating. The irony is that once the adolescent has spent years separating from his early family ties and is secure in his own independence he no longer wants to be separate. He is ready to merge his identity with that of someone else by creating a new, intense, one-to-one, love relationship.

The desire for a serious, long-lasting love relationship may begin as the end of adolescence draws near, or it may not be strongly felt until the person has reached his twenties or thirties. Psychologists are now aware that not everyone feels the same degree of need for intimacy, or at least for particular forms of intimacy. For example, until the women's movement of the 1960s and 1970s, it was assumed that all women wanted to marry young and raise families. Now we know that, although many women do want these things, others are equally interested in study or work and may be willing to postpone or forgo marriage or motherhood. Similarly, many young men hope to marry and settle down as soon as they are able to support a family financially, but others prefer to date more than one woman, at least for a while.

Our definitions of intimacy, and our expectations about it, are highly individual. But, if we allow for a broad range of individual variation, the fact remains that most people do experience a desire for a close, lasting, intimate love relationship. In contem-

A generation ago, it was generally assumed that when a woman reached adulthood she would become a wife and mother. Today, women enjoy more options. Many choose careers over motherhood.

porary Western society, that desire often, though not always, leads to marriage.

LIFE AND TIME

Some models of human development, such as the theories of Freud and Piaget discussed in Chapter 2, regard adulthood as the end point or final goal of growth. But other models, such as Erikson's, suggest that we never stop growing. In this view, our need for intimacy and our feelings about friendship and love do not arrive at a fixed point and then remain there, unchanging, throughout our adult lives. Instead, the process of living—as well as specific events that occur in individual lives—brings continuing changes to our intimate relationships.

For example, during adulthood we tend to experience intimate relationships with people of different generations. As children, we may have loving relationships with grandparents or other older people, but we are seldom able to communicate with them as equals or to understand them the way we understand our peers; young people who do share intimate, communicative relationships with older people are fortunate. As we mature, however, differences in age that once seemed huge appear to shrink. At 15, most people would find it difficult, if not impossible, to form a truly intimate friendship with a 40-year-old adult; at 30, however, a friendship with someone who is 55 does not seem so

Fortunate couples discover that their marriages become more meaningful as time passes.

improbable. One of the joys of growing up is discovering the possibility of genuine friendship, as well as familial love, with one's parents.

Aging also affects our relationships with our peers and loved ones. As teenagers, we tend to think that passionate love is a territory that belongs to hot-blooded youth. Adults, however, often discover that their marriages—as well as their friendships and relationships with other loved ones—become more and more precious and meaningful as years pass, particularly after retirement, when older people may no longer be occupied with raising a family or working. Couples and friends who grow old together can draw on a lifetime of mutual knowledge and shared experience, which is as great a treasure as any of us can hope to possess. And social scientists who have studied the elderly find that in many cases older people develop new social skills and actively seek out friends and companions to offset loneliness and isolation. Some studies, such as the one conducted by the California State Department of Health from 1982–83, have even indicated that intimacy prolongs health and life; people in their seventies who have regular contact with two or more friends or family members become ill less often and recover more quickly than those who feel themselves to be alone in the world. The California study concluded that "friends are good medicine."

All major life events, such as attending college, starting a career or a family, getting married, suing for divorce, or coping with the death of a loved one, can affect our appetite for intimacy and our ability to be a friend or a lover. Young people starting college or their first jobs often feel guilty and unhappy because they are devoting less time and energy to old friendships. New parents often find that, in the excitement and exhaustion of having a baby in their lives, they are making less time for each other. And on the death of a parent or close friend, some people reach out for support from others, but some people feel a need to withdraw from intimacy for a while in order to mourn privately.

We can obtain three valuable insights from looking at life as a constant process of development, with intimacy as part of that development. The first is that love, affection, and caring are not only sexual in nature. These feelings and impulses are born from our earliest life experiences, and we have the ability to apply them to as many people and relationships as we want.

The second valuable lesson is that life is not static; it does not stand still. If one semester we are desperately eager to be liked by someone at school, only to lose all interest in the relationship by the following semester, we need not be alarmed. From time to time, the amount and kind of intimacy we need changes, and so does our ability to achieve friendship and love.

The third valuable lesson is that, although the concept of individual development explains how our affections originate and grow, it does not set limits on them. In other words, intimacy is not like height—something fixed and measurable. If the whole world were to agree that five feet nine inches was the ideal height, some of us would be just right, but most of us would be considered either too tall or too short. And there would be nothing we could do about it. But, although most people agree that supportive friendships and enduring love relationships are the ideal of intimacy, those who have not achieved that goal are not doomed to be eternally unpopular, lonely, and unloved.

The skills of developing relationships and intimacy can be learned and improved upon. Self-help books, counseling, practice, the passage of time, and simple determination can bring about real changes in an individual's experience of friendship and love. Each of us has a unique life story of intimate relationships. The early chapters were written by our parents and families; during adolescence, we are coauthors with our parents and others around us; but as we enter adulthood, we are writing our own stories.

•   •   •   •

CHAPTER 5

· · · · · · · · · · · · · ·

MEN, WOMEN, AND INTIMACY

Love is a kind of warfare.

—*Ovid,* Ars Amatoria, *c. 1 B.C.E.*

From Shakespeare to stand-up comedians, people have compared the relationship between the sexes to combat, in which each side uses tricks, flattery, subtle schemes, or outright bullying to win what it wants from the other. This image of men and women at odds with one another is based on the idea that the two sexes are different in ways other than the obvious physical differences.

The notion of profound differences between the sexes came under fire in the middle of this century, as the women's movement gained strength and people reexamined traditional stereotypes— their beliefs and expectations—about the sexes. But studies have shown that there are indeed some fundamental differences between men and women. These differences do not apply to all individuals in the same degree. Nor do they mean that one sex is stronger, smarter, kinder, or better qualified to be a parent or a president than the other. They simply mean that, taken as a whole, each of the sexes exhibits some distinctive characteristics. These differences appear in early childhood and probably help shape our attitudes toward intimacy.

Boys tend to excel at activities that require speed, strength, coordination of large body movements (such as sports), and mechanical and mathematical comprehension. They also seem to be more aggressive and competitive than girls and to have a somewhat stronger drive toward individual achievement. Girls tend to excel at activities that require coordination of smaller movements (such as handcrafts), rapid comprehension and accurate memory, and skills of language and communication. They also seem to place a high value on cooperation and social harmony, and some studies suggest that social acceptance may be more important to girls than to boys.

These differences are not universal. Many girls are just as sports-oriented, competitive, and aggressive as boys and remain completely feminine. Similarly, a boy is no less masculine if he excels in language rather than math or behaves toward others with more cooperation than competition. There is plenty of room for individual variation. In addition, no one has been able to answer the vexing question of just how much of these differences is inborn and how much is formed by the attitudes and behavior of families and society in general. It is a well-established fact that gender (sex) differences are projected onto children from birth onward. Babies are dressed in blue if they are boys, in pink if they are girls. Young boys are generally expected to roughhouse and even fight a bit, and young girls are expected to act "ladylike."

This pattern continues through adulthood. Differences in be-

Contemporary society allows people to pursue their own interests. Young boys are not considered abnormal if they prefer the quiet joys of handicrafts to the competitive atmosphere of athletics.

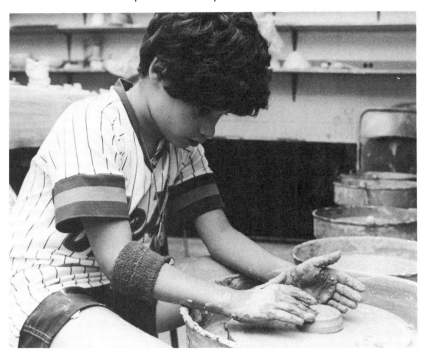

The spirit of competition is not exclusively a male domain. Young girls participate in sports with no loss of femininity.

havior and appearance are expected of males and females, and the majority of men and women usually do follow those expected patterns, at least in some ways. Which comes first—the behavior or the expectation? Do we follow certain patterns in life because society conditions us to do so, or does society simply reflect a fact of nature?

During the second half of the 20th century, particularly in the United States and Europe, widespread social changes have caused many people to grapple with these questions. Women have entered the workplace in large numbers and have demanded equality with men in professional and other employment opportunities and in pay. Divorce is increasingly common, and many men and women are single parents. Cultural values have changed, too; where once conformity was highly prized, today we are more tolerant of individuality, diversity, and flexibility. It is becoming more common for women to participate in sports and business and for men to take an active part in child rearing and homemaking. Many new parents plan to raise their children free from sex-role stereotypes. It will be interesting to see, in 20 years or so, whether society's images of men and women have changed, and whether men's and women's approaches to intimacy are different from those of today.

59

Increasingly, men are taking an active part in child rearing and home-making.

Differences in Friendship

In her 1985 book *Just Friends: The Role of Friendship in Our Lives,* psychologist Lillian Rubin reports the results of her own survey of men's and women's friendships, as well as of other sociological surveys and studies. She concludes that, in general, men and women tend to form very different kinds of friendships.

Girls are more likely to have one or more best friends early in life, whereas boys of the same age are more likely to identify with a group of buddies or casual friends. Later in life, men tend to produce longer lists of friends than women do, but most of those they cite as friends are people with whom they work, went to school, or play sports. Women, on the other hand, generally name fewer friends but regard most of them as closer and more intimate.

Both men and women meet friends in particular social situations or events, such as school, work, club meetings, sports

Homosexuality

Social scientists often divide human sexual behavior into three general categories: heterosexual, bisexual, and homosexual. Heterosexuals are attracted to members of the opposite sex. Bisexuals feel physically drawn to members of both sexes, although they may prefer one gender to the other. Homosexuality refers to the attraction one person feels for another of his or her own sex.

National surveys have yet to give a reliable account of the proportion of bisexuals in the overall population of the United States. But research indicates that about 10% of the nation's total population is homosexual and that the percentage has not changed since the first dependable statistics were released in the 1940s.

In recent years, many homosexuals have adopted the word gay to describe themselves, and the term has gained widespread acceptance. Many homosexual women, however, prefer to call themselves "lesbians," after the island of Lesbos, home of the ancient Greek poet Sappho, whose passionate verses—classics of Western literature—were addressed to other women.

In the last generation, homosexual men and women have found it easier to assert themselves as individuals with a right to peace and dignity.

Gays and lesbians demonstrate for equal rights in front of the White House in 1979.

Anthropologists, sociologists, and historians have determined that homosexuals have existed in almost every culture, though their status has varied in different times and places. Some cultures—the nomadic tribes of Mongolia and Tibet, certain Native American tribes, and some agricultural societies in Africa, among others—have respected homosexuals as shamans (spiritual leaders gifted with healing powers). In Nazi Germany, however, homosexuals were among the first slated for extermination in Hitler's death camps. Even after Allied forces liberated the camps at the end of World War II, homosexual inmates were often classified as criminals and reimprisoned.

In the United States, gays of both sexes are currently receiving mixed signals from the larger society, especially after the AIDS crisis focused public attention on the gay community. The incidence of verbal and physical assault on gays is on the rise, but so is support from concerned heterosexuals. In general, the greater visibility gays have attained has helped to dismantle stereotypes, thus enabling them to be viewed as individuals rather than as identical members of an alien group.

But this development is not as new as it may seem. Indeed, until recently, a person's sexual orientation was generally not a matter of public comment. The terms homosexual and heterosexual did not even come into existence until the late 19th century. Since then, open discussions of sexuality have become much more commonplace, and theorists continue to debate the origins of sexual identity. Today the field is dominated by two camps: "essentialists" (who believe sexuality to be innate) and "social constructionists," their op-

Many parents now openly support their homosexual children.

ponents (who believe societal factors determine sexuality).

A groundbreaking study of human sexuality was conducted over the course of many years by Alfred C. Kinsey, a zoologist at the University of Indiana who in 1948 published a survey, *Sexual Behavior in the Human Male,* followed five years later by *Sexual Behavior in the Human Female.* The "Kinsey Reports," as they came to be known, were based on exhaustive interviews with thousands of people who described their sexual activity. After coding and classifying their responses, Kinsey diagrammed the whole range of human sexual expression. At one extreme he placed exclusively heterosexual individuals, with exclusively homosexual individuals at the other. To the surprise of many readers, the majority of humanity fell somewhere in between, having experienced varying degrees of attraction to members of both sexes.

Such insights are valuable, but they offer scant comfort to a young adult struggling to sort out his or her own sexuality. Adolescence is a time of exploration and experimentation. It can prove an especially confusing time for teenagers who think they may be gay but feel intense peer pressure to be heterosexual. Fortunately, because of the advances of the gay liberation movement young adults need no longer face these challenges alone. Gay organizations exist on a national, state, and local level and can provide information, advice, and support. In most areas of the country, local telephone directories list gay hotlines and associations. If such numbers are unavailable, consult the National Gay Task Force, based in Washington, D.C., which can help locate the nearest gay services organization.

teams, and the like. The difference is that men's friendships often remain structured by those situations or events, whereas women's friendships tend to move into other areas of their lives. For example, two young men who become friends over a season of soccer practice may continue to hang around together before, during, and after games, or to watch games or talk about games together. At some point, their friendship may include other activities, but they are likely to think of each other for quite some time as "my buddy from the soccer team" rather than as "my friend Jack." But young women who become friends in similar situations are likely to visit each other's homes, talk on the telephone, and share other activities, such as going shopping or to the movies, even in the early stages of their friendship.

Boys and men, however, tend to organize their friendships around doing things together (a process sometimes called male bonding). Men usually think of themselves as part of a group of friends—although they may have individual best friends as well, they generally interact as a group, sharing experiences and jokes and competing in games and sports. Women tend more often to organize their friendships on a one-to-one basis and to share more intimate feelings.

Not all of our friendships follow this pattern, but many of them do. And these differences in relating to friends of the same sex also affect relationships with the opposite sex. For example, boys are sometimes scornful of their girlfriends' ability to talk to other girls for hours without, as a boy might put it, "really saying anything." Girls, on the other hand, sometimes feel frustrated because boys are more action-oriented and do not usually engage in as much conversation and sharing of feelings as other girls do. But it is becoming more and more common for adolescents to have friendships (as opposed to crushes or dating relationships) with members of the opposite sex. According to Rubin, men and women who do have opposite-sex friends seem better able to understand and communicate with their romantic partners. She also points out that many boys and men today admire the quality of emotional intimacy that exists in female friendships and hope to create some of the same supportive intimacy in their own friendships, just as many girls and women are adopting some of the competitive spirit and easygoing camaraderie of male friendships.

Women often have fewer friends than men, but their relationships tend to be more intimate.

Differences in Love

One stereotype about men and women holds that women are capable of loving just one man but men are naturally inclined to love more than one woman. This common belief is based on a confusion between love and sex. It is the case that most boys and men are able to become sexually aroused more quickly and by a greater number of people than most girls and women are. But although sexual arousal is part of love, love includes much else as well: trust, honesty, commitment, and sacrifice. Because most people hope for or demand faithfulness from their romantic partners, men and women alike must sacrifice a certain degree of freedom to act on their sexual impulses if they wish to protect their loving relationships. Love and sexual activity are powerful instinctive drives, but they are ultimately controlled by our conscious minds. Both men and women are quite capable of remaining faithful to a single loved one—or of delaying sexual activity until a secure, loving relationship exists.

In love relationships, as in friendship, people today are beginning to experiment and to borrow certain privileges and responsibilities that have traditionally belonged to the opposite sex. For example, it is quite common today for a girl to ask a boy for a date—something that used to be left entirely up to the boy. Although sex roles do play a vital part in developing our personalities and shaping our relationships, many men and women now feel greater freedom to express themselves and to communicate with each other in a wider variety of ways than their parents or grandparents did. There will always be differences between the sexes, but the differences do not have to mean that one way of relating to others is better or worse.

•   •   •   •

CHAPTER 6

A WORLD OF DIFFERENCES

Nothing venture, nothing win—
Blood is thick, but water's thin—
In for a penny, in for a pound—
It's Love that makes the world go round!

—*Sir William Schwenck Gilbert,* Iolanthe, *1882*

It may indeed be love that makes the world go round, as the saying goes, but as the world goes round, it reveals many different kinds of love. Friendship and intimacy are not at all the same things in all parts of the world or to all groups of people. In fact, the notions of friendship and love that seem common to most people in the Western world today are far from universal.

Even in the Western world, cultural differences abound. It is not uncommon, for example, for male friends in some European and Asian nations to express comradeship and affection by walking arm-in-arm, holding hands, or even kissing, all without necessarily suggesting homosexual overtones. Yet most English and American men would not feel comfortable with this sort of display—not because they are more manly or less friendly than, for example, French or Spanish men, but simply because the cultures from which they come regard such behavior differently.

The basic human drive toward interaction is universal. It fulfills a deep need to belong, to care and be cared for, to enjoy self-esteem and the esteem of others. But that basic, universal drive finds expression in countless ways. When the science of anthropology emerged in the 19th century, one of the first things anthropologists discovered was that the customs, practices, and beliefs that govern people's interactions with each other display an extraordinary range of diversity. These customs, practices,

Two Spanish men embrace. In many cultures, men commonly express affection with a kiss or hug.

and beliefs—sometimes grouped together and called *mores* (maw'-răz)—are part of each culture's heritage. And members of one culture are likely to be shocked, amused, horrified, or fascinated by what passes for normal in another culture.

Until recent decades, for example, the Hindu religion as practiced in India and the neighboring nation of Nepal required the wives in certain social classes to demonstrate their devotion to their husbands and their religious faith through the custom of *suttee*—allowing themselves to be burned alive on the funeral pyre of their dead husband. This custom was condemned by Europeans, and, as European ways gained influence in India, suttee was gradually abandoned and is now illegal. But many other mores involving love and friendship continue to preserve cultural differences.

Friendship Around the World

The nature of friendship depends upon the context in which it is found. Over much of the earth today (and during much of the history of all peoples), the struggle for existence means that individuals experience very little of the leisure time during which we often enjoy our friendships.

Among peoples who live by hunting, such as the American Indians of the far North, men associate not in sports or games but in the life-or-death business of survival. The bonds between them are formed not of shared pleasures but of mutual dependence and trust. Such peoples have developed rituals to strengthen these bonds. The huntsmen of many African tribes belong to secret, all-male societies. Some of these societies are simply the local version of social clubs, but many have religious or political purposes. Their primary purpose, however, is to create a sense of affiliation, or brotherhood, among the men of the community.

Another ritual that strengthens bonds among some primitive peoples is blood brotherhood, in which two unrelated men pledge to guard and support each other like brothers, often sealing the pledge with a ceremony such as mixing the blood from small, self-inflicted wounds. This ritual gives a formal structure, recognized by everyone in the society, to the relationship. Afterward, the blood brothers enjoy privileges and responsibilities like those that, in other societies, might exist between best friends. A version of blood brotherhood based on religious practice has developed in some Latin-American countries. Called *compadrazgo*, it is the tight-knit relationship between a father and the godfather of his child. To be chosen as a *compadre* is both a great honor and a great responsibility. In most countries, however, the sharing of blood to symbolize friendship is recognized as an extremely dangerous practice because many diseases may be contracted in this manner.

Military life somewhat resembles life in an early hunting society, and people who serve in the armed forces together often form intense, even ritualized bonds like those of blood brothers. Perhaps because soldiers are to some degree cut off from the mainstream of social and family life, they tend to emphasize the importance of their male bonds and of the military attitude. This military or warrior thinking is one of the sources of the attitude that is sometimes called macho, which endorses male toughness, competitiveness, and superiority. Many people today feel that, because most societies no longer exist in a state of constant war, the military-minded macho attitude has outlived its usefulness and hinders intimacy.

The women of many cultures, too, tend to form bonds among themselves based on the needs of day-to-day life. In villages and

The ghats along the Ganges River in India, where bodies are first dipped in water and then burned. In the past, it was not unknown for a Hindu woman to fling herself on her husband's burning funeral pyre.

farm communities, such as those that covered most of North America not long ago and are found today throughout Asia, Africa, and South America, women know that tasks such as sowing crops and sewing quilts will go more quickly when shared by a group. In urban environments, where industrial development has eliminated the need for everyone to work the soil for a living, the ancient forms of brotherhoods and sisterhoods live on in the sororities and fraternities of university life and the clubs, lodges, and other organizations of adult life.

Culture not only provides the context for friendship but tells us who can—and cannot—be our friends. Most village and farming communities in Africa, for example, are really large extended families. Although young men and women may marry people from different clans or villages, they are expected to form friendships and social relationships only within their own villages—and, indeed, they may have little opportunity to do otherwise unless they go away to school. And many cultures do not accept the idea of friendships between boys and girls, or even between adult men and women. Such relationships, if they come into being, are sometimes viewed as nonproductive and even potentially destructive. In Islamic cultures, tradition calls for boys and girls to be raised entirely apart. It is almost unheard of for a woman raised according to strict Muslim principles to have any but the most fleeting and superficial contact (bargaining for goods in a bazaar, perhaps) with men other than her father, brothers, uncles, husband, and sons. The bonds of friendship, family devotion, and sisterhood among Muslim women are said to be especially strong, as are the ties of brotherhood and friendship among men.

Love Around the World

Even more than friendship, love and sexual behavior show a large degree of variation from culture to culture. In fact, the strange and exotic sexual practices of far-off places have appealed to the popular imagination in many forms, from the tales of Marco Polo and other medieval travelers to the more scientific accounts of present-day anthropologists and *National Geographic* articles.

Even something as basic as which body parts are thought to be sexually attractive is capable of a wide variety of interpretations. For centuries, aristocratic Chinese men were fired with lust at the sight of the tiny, deformed, bound feet of upper-class women, because such feet were deemed attractive by traditional Chinese culture. The traditional garment of Indian women, the sari, exposes the midriff but covers the shoulders and upper back, an area of the body that Indians consider very sexy. In some African and Asian cultures, heavy people are considered attractive because weight suggests prosperity; in Europe and the United States, however, the current preferred shape for men and women is lean and muscular.

Physical expressions of sexual feeling vary, too. Among some peoples, including many Native American, African, and Polynesian cultures, lovers would never dream of kissing one another; the mouth is used for eating and drinking and is believed to have nothing to do with affection. And the story has often been told of how European and American missionaries, arriving in the

The Delights and Dangers of Anthropology

In the early years of the 20th century, when the science of cultural anthropology was maturing, a young Philadelphia woman named Margaret Mead (1901–78) studied anthropology at Columbia University in New York. Her professor was Franz Boas, perhaps the leading anthropologist of his time. Mead was just one of many students whom Boas fired with enthusiasm and sent out into the world to carry out field research. She spent 1925–26 in Samoa, a remote cluster of islands in the Pacific Ocean.

Mead's observations about the lives and customs of the Samoans led to exciting conclusions, which she published in 1928 under the title *Coming of Age in Samoa: A Psychological Study of Primitive Youth for Western Civilization.* Mead's book was one of the first written for a general audience to present the view that culture is variable and that what constitutes normal, acceptable behavior in New York may be quite different from normal, acceptable behavior in Samoa—and vice versa. In particular, she pointed out that the lively sexual behavior of Samoan adolescents, which might appear immoral to someone by Western standards, did not seem to have any ill effects on Samoan society, which she described as stable and happy.

Mead's book found an enormous readership and helped propel her to a well-deserved position of eminence as a leading anthropologist and social critic. For years it stood as a model of scientific methods and as a milestone in our understanding of the complexity and diversity of culture.

Then, in 1984, anthropologist Derek Freeman published *Margaret Mead and Samoa: The Making and Unmaking of a Myth.* In this highly controversial book, he claimed that Mead's observations of the Samoans had been flawed and that her conclusions were

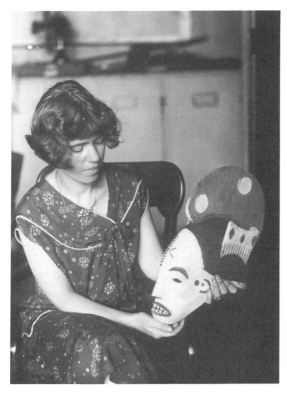

Anthropologist Margaret Mead in 1928, the year her book Coming of Age in Samoa: A Psychological Study of Primitive Youth for Western Civilization *was published.*

shaky. Freeman argued that Mead had been given dubious data by her Samoan friends, who with characteristic eagerness to please their visitor (who was as fascinating to them as they were to her) answered her questions in the way that they thought would most please her. He then suggested that Mead examined Samoan culture not with an open mind but with expectations and assumptions based on her studies with Boas and others. In short, he said, she found in Samoa just what she expected to find, not necessarily what was really there.

Other scholars leaped to Mead's defense, pointing out that Freeman was guilty of the very faults he saw in Mead. The scholarly storm has blown over, and the challenge to Mead has been largely dismissed. But the story of *Coming of Age in Samoa* suggests that, while we may acquire valuable insights and take great pleasure from the study of other cultures, we will remain in some sense forever outside them. Even our own cultural forces, especially the ones that shape our behavior in such intimate, powerful realms as friendship and love, are always going to be at least a little mysterious and elusive.

Hawaiian Islands, were scandalized to find that the islanders enjoyed having sex in more than one position. The missionaries claimed that only one way was correct—face to face, with the man on top, which came to be called the "missionary position."

Not only do sexual mores differ, but concepts of love and marriage differ as well. In much of the world, in fact, the idea of romantic love and marriage that is so common in the Western world simply does not exist. In Muslim cultures and in Asia, most marriages are based not on a passionate love that draws two people together and causes them to choose each other as life partners, but on family decisions. Marriages are arranged for young people, sometimes while they are still children, and it is not uncommon for them not to meet one another until the day of their betrothal (formal engagement) or even their wedding.

Some of these marriages are arranged on the advice of astrologers or spiritual advisers, as in India, where the horoscopes of a potential couple are cast to determine whether the marriage will be a favorable one. In Japan, an individual called a *nahodo* arranges traditional marriages. The nahodo searches out possible mates for a young man or woman and evaluates their education, family status, and income. If both families approve of the match, they announce that the young people are joined in a *miai*, or

In China, women field-workers toil side by side. Women in many farming cultures share their tasks in order to speed up their workday.

formal betrothal, that will be followed by a wedding. In modern Japan, however, both men and women have been influenced by Western notions of romantic love and individual choice, and some matches are made by young people themselves, who observe the traditional forms as a matter of respect. The nahodo has become less a marriage broker and more an introduction service, and the miai is now often a dating relationship rather than a strict engagement; young Japanese men and women may try a series of miai before settling on a marriage partner.

Arranged marriages often have an economic basis. Among the many cattle-herding Bantu peoples of Africa, custom calls for a young man who wishes to marry to pay a bride-price in cattle to the father of his chosen bride. The European and early American tradition was just the opposite: The father of the bride was expected to provide her with a dowry in cash or goods with which to start life with her husband. That custom persists in the tradition that the family of the bride will pay for the wedding.

Despite all this variety, most cultures have customs or laws that control, in some way or another, the following four basic aspects of love and sexuality.

Marriage Nearly all societies have some form of approved marriage. This form may be monogamy (marriage to one person at a time), as in Europe and the United States, or some type of polygamy (marriage to more than one person at a time). A Muslim man is permitted by his religious and civil laws to be polygynous—that is, to have more than one wife (as many as four, if he can afford it). Among some Tibetan and Central Asian peoples, women may be polyandrous (married to two or more men, usually brothers). In addition to formal marriage, some cultures recognize common-law marriage, in which a man and woman who live together and have children are considered to have the same responsibilities and rights as married people. Another widely recognized type of relationship is concubinage, in which a woman is acknowledged as a man's mistress and is expected to behave toward him as a wife would, although he may be married to another woman. In traditional Asian cultures, concubines often shared the house of the wife and husband, and their children were sometimes adopted by the married couple.

These relationships serve a universally recognized social pur-

A wedding ceremony in Japan, where marriages are often arranged by a nahodo, *or matchmaker.*

pose. Without them, men and women would be endlessly involved in competition for mates and in courtship. By assuring people of sexual and social partners, marriage (or its equivalent) enables them to devote energy and attention to the other tasks of life, such as work and child rearing.

Consent The second aspect of sexual behavior governed by most cultures concerns willing and unwilling sexual partners. Although contemporary Americans might view with dismay the prospect of a 14-year-old girl, without any say in the matter, being married to a stranger, such marriages are acceptable in the cultures in which they occur. But every culture recognizes situations in which forcing others to have sex is wrong. Nearly all societies have taboos, or strong cultural prohibitions, against sex with children and against rape.

Endogamy and Exogamy Every culture sets up guidelines as to whom an individual may marry or choose as a sexual partner. A young man or woman can marry either endogamously (within a group, such as a race, nationality, religion, social class, or clan, to which he or she belongs) or exogamously (into another group). Most societies practice a mixture of endogamy and exogamy. For example, Indians marry only within the rather rigid lines of economic, religious, and professional classes, or castes, that structure Indian society; for a man or woman to choose someone above or below his or her caste is shameful for both. Europeans and Americans, however, may smile with approval when a son or daughter wishes to marry someone from a wealthier background but be considerably less enthusiastic when the choice falls on someone of a poorer background or of a different religion or race.

One taboo that is found in virtually every society is incest, or sexual relations between family members. Of course, the definition of *family* is variable. An Arab, for example, may marry his brother's wives in order to support them after his brother is killed, but such marriages are forbidden in some Asian cultures. Nearly all cultures ban sexual or marital relations between siblings or between parents and their children.

Such a ban exists not only for moral reasons, but for health ones as well. Marriage between two siblings, a parent and a child, or even first cousins poses great genetic risks to their offspring. Children born of these relationships have a greater chance of being born with a host of diseases parents can pass on to their children, including hemophilia (a blood disease in which the clotting agent in the blood is defective or missing). It is also believed that inbreeding can produce children who are mentally handicapped and born with any number of physical deformities as well. In fact, some scientists believe that the reason for the elongated heads we see in much of Egyptian art is that many members of the royal Egyptian families married within their own family. In more recent history, the royal Romanov family of pre-communist Russia was plagued with hereditary hemophilia as a result of generations of intermarriage.

Scientists now believe, however, that although there are a number of medical risks involved with intermarriage within the same family, they may not be as severe as once believed, and that it is more likely that the incest taboo exists more for moral than medical reasons.

Exceptions The fourth way in which societies govern love and marriage is by providing for exceptions to the prevailing rules. It is generally acknowledged that human beings find it difficult to live up to their ideals, especially when such powerful drives as love and sex are involved. So most societies allow people to bend the rules in certain ways. One such way is divorce. A very few societies do not permit divorce, and in some societies a man may divorce his wife but she may not divorce him. Nevertheless, some legally and socially acceptable way to dissolve a marriage is found in most societies where marriage occurs. Another kind of exception is prostitution, which is regarded as a trade like any other in some parts of the world. Even where it is officially discouraged by law or religion, it usually appears in some form.

•   •   •   •

CHAPTER 7

. . . .

INTIMACY PAST AND PRESENT

Wherever you are, it is your own
friends who make your world.

—*William James from* The Thought and Character of
  William James, *Ralph Barton Perry, 1899*

That Love is all there is, Is all we know of Love. . . .

—*Emily Dickinson*

Different cultures express feelings of friendship and love in a multitude of ways, yet many of these ways are changing. Because the nations of the modern Western world—the United States, the Soviet Union, and the European countries—have played a dominant role in much of world history and politics during the past century, the cultural mores of those nations have been carried around the globe. In many countries, friendship and love are being shaped by the modern Western concept of romantic love, which is based on ideas of individual choice, personal happiness, and growth.

People—especially young people—in many countries are not only studying English and wearing jeans but also reading European books and watching American movies. Consequently, they are adopting some Western mores. Young single people in the People's Republic of China now go on dates and even hold hands in public, behavior that would have been frowned upon and perhaps punished a decade ago. Young people in India and Japan are asking to choose their own mates. More and more women in South America and Saudi Arabia want to go to college and have careers, which means that they are more likely to choose their own husbands, to marry later than their parents did, and possibly to have smaller families. These patterns of change are similar to changes that occurred in the West and gave rise to today's ideas about friendship and love.

THE HISTORY OF FRIENDSHIP AND LOVE

Some of the earliest civilizations in the West had ideas about love that we would consider quite unromantic today. To the Egyptians, the Greeks, and the Romans, love and marriage were two separate things. Marriage was a social and economic enterprise, designed to produce a household and a family. It was either arranged by a couple's parents or entered into like a well-understood social contract: Each partner was expected to give certain things, and each partner could expect to receive certain things in return. Passion, self-fulfillment, and intimacy did not carry much weight, although surely they did appear in many marriages. But love in marriage was usually a lucky by-product, not a universal expectation. People were expected to feel duty, loyalty, responsibility, and perhaps affection for their marriage partners. Passionate exaltation—falling in love—was sometimes a calamity, for it was just as easy for a man or woman to fall in love with the wrong person as the right one.

To these cultures, passionate, romantic love was a dangerous aberration that threatened to overturn the orderly life of the individual and of society. It was a kind of madness. The Greeks called this potentially destructive force *eros*, after the god Eros, who was the son of Aphrodite, goddess of beauty and love. (Later in history, the image of Eros was transformed into Cupid, the infant god who mischievously shoots mortals with arrows of love.) Our word *erotic* (passionate or sexual) comes from this word.

The Greeks tried to control eros by regarding marriage as a social obligation rather than a form of personal expression. In fact, the men of ancient Greece experienced their deepest and most important emotional feelings for other men. Homosexuality was common, even among married men, because men believed that women were not their equals and that they could share the joys of love, philosophy, and art only with their equals, who happened to be other men. (It would be interesting to know how the women of ancient Greece felt about all this, but their thoughts have not been preserved.)

Although the element of homosexuality in Greek relationships was never universal and was a short episode in the total span of history, it did leave some profound influences on Western thought. For one thing, it introduced the concept of a close, intimate relationship between men. Once the element of homosexual love faded, this concept became the ideal of friendship, as illustrated in the legend of Damon and Pythias.

Pythias was condemned to death as punishment for rebelling against the king. He asked for permission to make a final visit to his distant home, and his friend Damon offered his own life as a pledge that Pythias would return. But Pythias did not return, and as the day of Damon's death drew near, the king taunted him, saying, "You were a fool to believe that your friend would keep his promise and come back to face the executioner. He'll

The legend of Damon and Pythias exemplifies the trust and self-sacrifice found in most true friendships.

let you die instead. That's human nature!" On execution day, Pythias rushed up, full of fear that he had been delayed too long on the road and that Damon was dead. The two made an affectionate and dignified farewell, and Pythias stepped forward to face his fate. But the king was so moved by their devotion that he said, "If only I had a friend such as each of you has," and he pardoned Pythias. For centuries, the story of Damon and Pythias was a popular symbol of the trust and spirit of self-sacrifice that lie at the heart of true friendships.

Even though they distrusted passionate love, the philosophers of ancient Greece did speculate about the nature and meaning of love. Plato developed the theory that earthly love is merely a weak imitation of an ideal, or spiritual, love. The reality of love, he claimed, lay in the world of ideas, not the flesh-and-blood world. For this reason, we sometimes use the word platonic to describe a friendship or love relationship that does not include sexuality, as when a man and a woman who are friends but not lovers explain, "It's just platonic."

Christian Spiritual Love

The rise of Christianity in the ancient world introduced a new concept of love. The Greeks called it *agape;* the Romans called it *caritas;* and it is usually translated into English as *charity.* This form of love was one of the three chief Christian virtues (the others were faith and hope). The doctrine of charity, or compassion, preached that we should strive to feel universal, humanitarian love for all fellow human beings. This type of love is nonsexual, even impersonal. It is a service to God or to one's ideals, not to oneself.

Many people feel that, because of its selflessness and its religious impulse, spiritual love is the highest and best kind of love we can experience. Some of our cultural heroes illustrate the power of spiritual love. One of these is Dr. Albert Schweitzer (1875–1965), a German musician and student of religion who, at age 30, dedicated his life to serving as a medical missionary in Africa, where he built a hospital and a home for victims of leprosy. Another ideal of spiritual love is found in Mother Teresa (b. 1910), an Albanian woman who became a Catholic nun and, at 18, sailed to India to begin a lifetime of nursing in the crowded and poverty-stricken slums of Calcutta. The order she founded,

Dr. Albert Schweitzer spent his life serving as a medical missionary in Africa.

the Missionaries of Charity, now operates more than 200 medical missions around the world.

Courtly and Romantic Love

In the Middle Ages, the Western concept of love took a new turn. The two ideas of spiritual love and sexual love were fused in the concept called *courtly love*, which first appeared in the love poetry of southern France in the 11th century. Courtly love was modeled on the political structure of feudal kingdoms. In feudal kingdoms, there was a lord who ruled over the whole manor (a self-contained village) and was served by various classes of people, down to the lowly serfs, who tilled the land and were treated as slaves.

In courtly love, the man puts himself in the position of a vassal or underling who swears his devotion to—and is ruled by—the lord of the manor, in this case, his mistress. But courtly love also contained some religious elements. The beloved lady was often described as a saint, and the lover as a pilgrim who comes to her shrine to worship at her feet.

Courtly love had nothing to do with marriage. It was a literary and social phenomenon of the upper classes, and it took the form of passionate, secret relationships between people who were usually married to others. In many cases, the woman who was adored by a courtly lover never even knew him, for these grand passions were not meant to be acted on, but instead, to serve as inspirations for great deeds. For example, Beatrice, the young woman who was the object of the Italian poet Dante's lifelong courtly passion, appears in his poems as his spiritual guide through the realms of heaven and hell and as the ideal image of beauty. In real life, however, she was married to another man, and Dante is believed to have had a mistress and possibly several children.

Like the Greeks and Romans, the Europeans of the Middle Ages, even while they were drawn to the idea of passion, feared it as a destructive force. It is for this reason that the greatest tales of courtly love end badly for the lovers. Once they stop fantasizing about their passions and act on them in the real world, disaster follows. Lancelot's illicit love affair with Guinevere, the wife of his king, Arthur, brings about the downfall of Camelot, Arthur's court. Another famous medieval love story is that of Tristram and Isolde. Isolde is betrothed to Mark, Tristram's king. Against all the rules of good behavior for their society and era, Isolde

Perhaps the best-known living practitioner of selfless spiritual love is Mother Teresa.

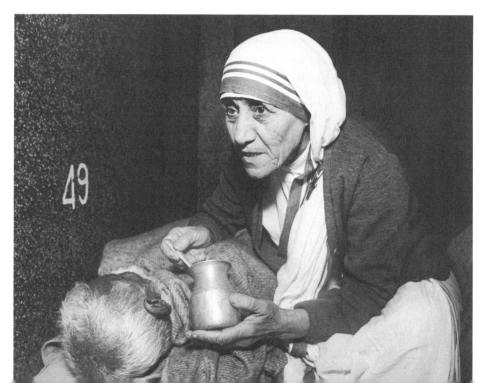

and Tristram fall in love. Tristram is killed, and Isolde kills herself over his body. The disruptive passion of Tristram and Isolde is blamed upon a magic love potion that they drink by mistake.

Such potions (or love charms) appear in the folklore and literature of many peoples. In fact, mankind has searched for centuries for a true *aphrodisiac* (named for the Greek goddess of love, Aphrodite, an aphrodisiac is any substance or object that is reputed to cause sexual desire). Scientists tell us, however, that no such thing exists. Two chemical substances (cantharides, which is extracted from insects, and yohimbine, which is extracted from the bark of an African tree) do stimulate sexual excitement in humans—but only when they are taken in such large doses that they are also poisonous. It is sometimes thought that alcohol and certain other drugs are aphrodisiacs, but this is not the case. These intoxicants merely diminish our self-control and inhibitions; they do not produce true sexual excitement.

The doomed, tragic image of courtly love persisted for several centuries. It appears in Shakespeare's 16th century play *Romeo and Juliet*, the tale of young lovers from feuding families who come to a tragic end. (Transported to 20th-century New York City, this story was the basis for the play and movie *West Side Story*.) But if we read Shakespeare's play carefully, we can see an important difference between it and other stories of courtly love.

In earlier tales, such as those of Lancelot and Guinevere and Tristram and Isolde, the lovers may have been inspired and passionate but they were also wrong, and they knew it. They had violated the accepted codes of behavior, and it was appropriate that they should die. But in *Romeo and Juliet*, Shakespeare ennobles his ill-fated lovers. Although they die, their deaths are seen not as their fault but as society's fault. At the end of the play, the ruler of their city acknowledges this when he says that he hopes the feud between their families will now end. Romeo and Juliet are indeed at odds with their society, but the conclusion of the play and, usually, of the reader is that the lovers are fine—society must change. This is a big departure from earlier concepts of love. It signals the beginning of a way of looking at love and friendship that still affects us today. That new image has come to be called romantic love.

Romantic love glorifies individual feelings, needs, desires, and experiences. In this view of human relationships, love is seen as

Romeo and Juliet *is a classical representation of romantic love as an exalted condition that prizes feelings, needs, and desires.*

an end in itself, not as a means to the end of social order. Desire is a more powerful and admirable force than duty. The romantic concept of relationships took further shape in the literature of the late 18th and early 19th centuries, for example in the poems of English writers such as William Blake and Lord Byron. Within the next century the new disciplines of psychology and psychiatry began to focus on personal development and fulfillment. At the same time, women began to demand and receive greater rights at school and in the workplace, which allowed greater numbers of men and women than ever before to meet as equals. As a result of all of these gradual processes, most of Western society today is influenced by the concept of romantic love, with its emphasis on independence, individual choice, diversity of relationships, and growth.

MODERN FRIENDSHIP

Some psychologists and social observers say that friendship is more important today than ever before. We live in a mobile world, where families often live far from the grandparents and other relatives who provided a supportive network of kinship to earlier generations. Families are smaller, too, and many marriages end in divorce. As a result, not everyone has a complete family of father, mother, and children under the same roof and other relatives within call. Religion, too, which was once a traditional source of comfort and support, is less meaningful to many people today.

Confronted with these changing social patterns, people find that life can be lonely at times. As a result, they turn more and more to their friends. For many people, relationships with friends meet needs that might once have been met in family life or marriage. Friends travel together, celebrate holidays and special rituals together, nurse and comfort each other during bad times, and share the pleasures of good times.

Along with the increasing importance of friendship in modern lives goes the fact that we are now able to make more friendships with more kinds of people than ever before in history. Communication with distant friends is easier than it has ever been. It is now more acceptable for friendships to exist between people of different sexes, races, and ages than it was in the past. But some psychologists feel that we know even less about friendship than we know about love.

We do know that there are many different kinds of friendship. Sometimes, in fact, we have trouble sorting out the different types of friendship in our lives. We are troubled when a friendship does not work out the way it "ought" to, yet perhaps our expectations are too narrow.

The Road and the Heart

Psychologist Lillian Rubin makes a useful and beautiful distinction between two types of friends. She calls them "friends of the road" and "friends of the heart."

Friends of the road are people whose lives touch ours, sometimes briefly, sometimes for longer periods, but always for a limited time. Friends of the road can be close friends indeed—we may see them every day and share the details of our lives with them. They can be neighbors, people we go to school or work with, or people we meet through any of the circumstances of our lives. Yet when the circumstances change, the friendships change, too. They require effort to keep up and they usually end sooner or later, after a few years' worth of Christmas cards have been exchanged. Somehow these one-time friends do not seem as important to us once they are not present in our lives on a regular basis.

By the time we reach adolescence, most of us have had the experience of seeing a close friendship end. Often we feel guilt and ask ourselves, "Why didn't I stay in touch with so-and-so?" or "What could I have done to keep this friendship alive?" But in many cases, friendships have a natural life cycle of birth, growth, fading, and death. These are friendships of the road, and if we can understand their nature and accept their limitations, they can bring us a great deal of joy and comfort. But they are not the same as friends of the heart.

Friends of the heart are our core friendships, the long-lasting and continuous relationships that travel through life with us and become part of us. Friendships of the heart keep themselves alive, even when the friends are separated for long periods. These friendships renew themselves because they are based on trust, intimacy, and the special bond of love that exists between friends who know and accept one another fully. Friendships of the heart can survive crises that would destroy friendships of the road.

One famous example of a true friendship of the heart existed between John Adams of Massachusetts and Thomas Jefferson of Virginia during the early years of the United States. The two patriots met during the excitement of the American Revolution and worked together on the Declaration of Independence. A close friendship, based on mutual esteem and shared ideals, sprang up between the two. Later in their lives, however, political differences came between them and caused a deep estrangement that lasted for many years. Later still, when both were old and retired, they renewed a correspondence that had been broken off years before. To their delight, they discovered that the passage of time had erased many of their differences, but the respect and affection they had once felt for one another remained intact. They embarked on a vigorous and stimulating exchange of letters that lasted for several decades and that became, for both men, one of the sustaining joys of their later lives. By a curious and touching coincidence, they died on the same day, the 50th anniversary of Independence Day.

Friendship takes many forms today. It may be a casual acquaintanceship, as with someone we smile at or say hello to in passing. It may be a friendship based on certain activities, or limited to a certain time period. A special type of friendship that often forms at school or work and that is based on respect and sharing is the relationship between a mentor (an experienced guide or teacher who helps a younger person develop) and a protégé (who learns from the mentor). Finally, there is the intimate, enduring friendship of the heart. We cannot expect all friendships to be all things, nor can we reasonably expect to enjoy all kinds of friendships at all times. But each friendship, however large or small, has the potential for enriching not just one but two lives.

MODERN LOVE

Some aspects of love in today's world have had a tremendous effect on everyone, especially on young people who are in the process of discovering love. We would all like to believe that love, once found, is eternal; statistics, however, tell us that half of all marriages in the United States today will end in divorce. Teenagers today are supposed to have the benefits of enlightened sex education, yet teenage pregnancy rates are soaring, and the emotional and financial cost to the nation—especially to the teen mothers and their infants—is enormous. The sexual revolution of the late 1960s and the 1970s was supposed to usher in an era of open, sane, healthy sexuality; but today we have a growing number of people who admit that mere sex is unsatisfying and that they long for more meaningful romantic relationships.

On top of everything else, sexually transmitted diseases (STDs) are more prevalent than ever before. The deadly disease AIDS has been in the spotlight of public attention in recent years, but doctors report a rise in other STDs, including gonorrhea, syphilis, herpes, and genital warts, a form of viral infection that may be related to cervical cancer. These sexually related health problems are growing rapidly in the adolescent population. Every teenager, whether or not he or she is sexually active, should try to learn the facts about pregnancy and STDs from a reliable source— such as the U.S. government brochure called "Understanding AIDS"—and to act on those facts. Making a mistake concerning sexual behavior is more serious than ever.

Today, adolescents have access to more information about sex, love, and friendship than ever before. Self-help books by the thousands fill the shelves of our bookstores, offering us tips on how to win friends, love and be loved, and overcome loneliness. Television movies regularly dramatize such issues as homosexuality, pregnancy, and AIDS. Many schools and community health centers offer courses or information on making friends, planning for marriage and family, or prevention of STDs. Yet despite this glut of information, friendship and love remain as challenging—and at the same time as simple and natural—as they have always been.

Intimacy, whether emotional or sexual or both, is always a test of maturity and responsibility. To succeed at intimacy, an individual must be honest about his or her feelings, true to his or her values, and generous with his or her inner self. But friendship and love are well worth the effort; some people say they are the crowning experiences of our lives. The English Romantic poet John Keats said, describing all human experiences and virtues, that

> the crown of these
> Is made of love and friendship, and sits high
> Upon the forehead of humanity.

APPENDIX:

FOR MORE INFORMATION

The following is a list of organizations that can provide additional information regarding some of the issues covered in *Friendship and Love* or recommend other agencies that can be of further assistance.

CULTURAL STUDIES

American Anthropological
  Association
1703 New Hampshire Avenue, N.W.
Washington, D.C. 20009
(202) 232-8800
(publishes 12 professional journals
  in areas ranging from medical to
  educational anthropology)

FAMILY

American Academy of Family
  Physicians
1740 W. 92nd Street
Kansas City, MO 64114
(816) 333-9700

American Academy of Natural
  Family Planning
615 South New Ballas Road
St. Louis, MO 63141
(314) 569-6295

Center for Population Options
1012 14th Street, N.W., Suite 1200
Washington, D.C. 20005
(202) 347-5700

CHOICE
c/o Women's Way
125 South Ninth Street, Suite 603
Philadelphia, PA 19107
(215) 592-7644

Family Health International
Triangle Drive
Research Triangle Park, NC 27709
(919) 549-0517

Family Resource and Referral
  Center Hotline
(612) 331-2776

Family Service Association of
  America
44 E. 23rd Street
New York, NY 10010
(212) 674-6100

Institute of Marriage and Family
  Relations
6116 Rolling Road, Suite 316
Springfield, VA 22152
(703) 569-2400

National Council on Family
  Relations
1219 University Avenue SE
Minneapolis, MN 55414
(612) 331-2774

National Organization of
  Adolescent Pregnancy and
  Parenting
P.O. Box 2365
Reston, VA 22090
(703) 435-3948

Planned Parenthood Federation of
  America
810 Seventh Avenue
New York, NY 10019
(212) 541-7800

HOMOSEXUALITY

Association for Gay and Lesbian
  Issues in Counseling
Box 216
Jenkintown, PA 19046
(Its referral network is available to
  counselors, administrators, and
  teens.)

Fund for Human Dignity
666 Broadway, 4th Floor
New York, NY 10012
(212) 529-1600
(operates a national clearinghouse
  of educational materials on
  gay/lesbian- and AIDS-related
  issues)

Homosexual Information Center
6758 Hollywood Boulevard, Suite
  208
Hollywood, CA 90028
(213) 464-8431

Institute for the Protection of
  Lesbian and Gay Youth
110 East 23rd Street, 10th Floor
New York, NY 10010
(212) 473-1113

Lesbian Resource Center
1212 East Pine Street
Seattle, WA 98122

National Federation of Parents and
  Friends of Gays
8020 Eastern Avenue, N.W.
Washington, DC 20009
(202) 332-6483

YOUTH

Allied Youth and Family
  Counseling Center
P.O. Box 801412
Dallas, TX 75380
(214) 934-2234

Youth Counseling League
138 E. 19th Street
New York, NY 10003
(212) 473-4300
(an outpatient counseling clinic for
  adolescents and young adults)

FURTHER READING

Alberoni, Francesco. *Falling in Love*. Translated by Lawrence Venuti. New York: Random House, 1983.

Asher, Steven R., and John A. Arieti. *The Development of Children's Friendships*. Cambridge, England: Cambridge University Press, 1981.

Bellah, Robert N., et al. *Habits of the Heart: Individualism and Commitment in American Life*. New York: Harper & Row, 1986.

Bloch, Joel D. *Friendship*. New York: Macmillan, 1976.

Branden, Nathaniel. *The Psychology of Romantic Love*. New York: Bantam Books, 1981.

Brazelton, T. Berry. *Becoming a Family: The Growth of Attachment*. New York: Delacorte Press, 1981.

Engstrom, Ted W. *The Fine Art of Friendship: Building and Maintaining Quality Relationships*. New York: Thomas Nelson Publishers, 1985.

Erikson, Erik H. *Childhood and Society*. New York: Norton, 1950.

Fromm, Erich. *The Art of Loving: An Enquiry into the Nature of Love*. New York: Harper & Row, 1962.

Gaylin, Willard. *Rediscovering Love*. New York: Penguin Books, 1987.

Staff of the *Jerusalem Post*. *Anatoly and Avital Scharansky: The Journey Home*. New York: Harcourt Brace Jovanovich, 1986.

Keen, Sam. *The Passionate Life: Stages of Loving*. San Francisco: Harper & Row, 1983.

Kennedy, Eugene. *On Being a Friend*. New York: Continuum, 1982.

Liebowitz, M. R. *The Chemistry of Love*. Boston: Little, Brown 1983.

Madaras, Lynda. *Lynda Madaras' Growing-Up Guide for Girls*. New York: Newmarket Press, 1986.

Maslow, Abraham. *Motivation and Personality*. New York: Harper & Row, 1954.

———. *Religion, Values, and Peak Experiences*. New York: Viking Press, 1970.

Mead, Margaret. *Coming of Age in Samoa: A Psychological Study of Primitive Youth for Western Civilization*. 1928. Reprint. New York: Morrow, 1973.

Michealis, David. *The Best of Friends: Profiles of Extraordinary Friendships*. New York: Morrow, 1983.

Naylor, Phyllis Reynolds. *Getting Along with Your Friends*. Nashville, TN: Abingdon Press, 1980.

Newton, James. *Uncommon Friends*. New York: Harcourt Brace Jovanovich, 1987.

Nonkin, Lesley Jane. *I Wish My Parents Understood*. New York: Penguin Books, 1985.

Parkes, Colin Murray, and John Stevenson-Hinde. *The Place of Attachment in Human Behavior*. New York: Basic Books, 1982.

Piaget, Jean, and Barbel Inhelder. *The Psychology of the Child*. New York: Basic Books, 1969.

Pomeroy, Wardell B. *Girls & Sex*. New York: Dell, 1981.

Rubin, Lillian B. *Just Friends: The Role of Friendship in Our Lives*. New York: Harper & Row, 1985.

Simmel, George. *On Women, Sexuality, and Love*. Translated by Guy Oakes. New Haven: Yale University Press, 1984.

Teilhard de Chardin, Pierre. *On Love and Happiness*. San Francisco: Harper & Row, 1984.

Tennov, Dorothy. *Love and Limerance: The Experience of Being in Love*. New York: Stein & Day, 1979.

GLOSSARY

AIDS acquired immune deficiency syndrome; an acquired defect in the immune system, thought to be caused by a virus (HIV) and contracted by blood or sexual contact; leaves people vulnerable to certain, often fatal, infections and cancers

anthropology the study of the cultural, physical, and social development of humans

aphrodisiac any substance or object that is reputed to cause sexual desire

attachment a child's unconscious dependency on its primary caretaker

betrothal formal engagement for marriage

bisexuality human sexual behavior in which a person is attracted to members of both sexes

charity a spiritual form of love that is universal, humanitarian, and nonsexual; as one of three chief Christian virtues, this quality signifies service to God or to one's ideals, not to oneself

compadrazgo a version of blood brotherhood based on religious practices found in some Latin-American countries involving a father and the godfather of his child

concubinage societally sanctioned relationship between the sexes in which a woman is acknowledged as a man's mistress and is expected to fulfill the duties of a wife, although he may be married to another woman

courtly love the spiritual love characteristic of medieval nobility, often manifested in literature and modeled after the political structures of feudal kingdoms; the male enacts the role of a vassal or underling who swears devotion to his mistress; this type of relationship took the form of passionate, secret relationships between people usually married to others

crush an intense, often one-sided infatuation that is not usually acted upon

ego integrity satisfaction with oneself and one's life; the positive force in stage eight of Erik Erikson's model of human development

endogamy marriage within a group

Erikson's model model of human growth not limited to childhood and adolescence but representing a lifelong process with eight stages; each stage can be viewed as a conflict between two opposing forces; one promoting healthy mental, emotional, and social growth, the other stunting growth

eros passionate, romantic love named after the Greek god of sexual love, Eros

exogamy marriage outside of a group

generativity giving or creating something new; the positive force in stage seven of Erikson's model

genital warts condylomae; fleshy growths occurring in and around the genitals and anus in both sexes and sexually transmitted by the human papilloma virus (HPV)

heterosexuality human sexual behavior in which members of the opposite sex are the primary objects of sexual desire; i.e., women are sexually attracted to men and men to women

hierarchy of needs Abraham Maslow's ranking of universal human needs such that no level can be attained without fulfillment of the need preceding it

homosexuality human sexual behavior in which members of the same sex are the primary objects of desire

incest sexual intercourse between closely related persons

individuation the stage of psychological development in which a child becomes more aware of himself as an individual being, apart from his mother, and gradually takes more responsibility for himself

intimacy a shared feeling of closeness between people

limerance the exciting time at the beginning of a new relationship when the attraction is strong and the partners are in the process of discovering one another; coined by Dorothy Terrov, the term describes the process of falling in love that may, but will not necessarily, lead to a lasting love relationship

macho an exaggerated sense of or pride in masculinity emphasizing male toughness, competitiveness, and superiority

miai the formal Japanese betrothal that precedes a wedding

monogamy marriage to one person at a time

mores customs, practices, and beliefs common to a culture's heritage

nahado in Japan, an individual who arranges traditional marriages

papyrus a scroll of paper made from papyrus reed, used by Egyptians to record economic transactions and history and to inscribe literature

physiological development physical, measurable growth

Piaget's model outline primarily of childhood intellectual growth; divided into four stges, this model claims that emotional, social, and physical development occur with the growth of mental abilities

platonic description for a friendship or love relationship that does not include sexuality

pleasure principle Freud's term for the human tendency to seek immediate satiation of desires

polyandry marriage to more than one man at a time

polygamy marriage to more than one person at a time

polygyny marriage to more than one woman at a time

preadolescence the period of development immediately prior to adolescence, or puberty

psychological development growth of intellectual and affective capacities, marked by changes in emotional and mental processes

psychology the study of mental processes and behavior

puberty the period of approximately two years during which the body's reproductive system becomes physically mature, occurring around the age of 12 to 13 in girls and 13 to 14 in boys

reality principle Freud's term for a child's gradual realization that the world does not provide the immediate satisfaction of instinctual drives demanded by the pleasure principle

sociology the study of human social behavior and societies

STD sexually transmitted disease

suttee a ritual now forbidden but once practiced in Indian and Nepalese Hinduism in which a wife shows religious faith and devotion to her deceased spouse by burning herself to death on his funeral pyre

INDEX

PICTURE CREDITS

Rebecca Stefoff is a Philadelphia-based author and editor who has written more than 25 nonfiction books, many of them for young-adult readers. She holds a Ph.D. in English from the University of Pennsylvania, where she taught from 1974 to 1977. She recently completed a two-year term as editor in chief for TLC, a health-oriented magazine for hospital inpatients, currently serves as editorial director of the Chelsea House series PLACES AND PEOPLES OF THE WORLD, and has contributed the volumes *Arafat* and *King Faisal* to the Chelsea House series WORLD LEADERS.

Dale C. Garell, M.D., is medical director of California Childrens Services, Department of Health Services, County of Los Angeles. He is also clinical professor in the Department of Pediatrics and Family Medicine at the University of Southern California School of Medicine and Visiting associate clinical professor of maternal and child health at the University of Hawaii School of Public Health. From 1963 to 1974, he was medical director of the Division of Adolescent Medicine at Children's Hospital in Los Angeles. Dr. Garell has served as president of the Society for Adolescent Medicine, chairman of the youth committee of the American Academy of Pediatrics, and as a forum member of the White House Conference on Children (1970) and White House Conference on Youth (1971). He has also been a member of the editorial board of the *American Journal of Diseases of Children.*

C. Everett Koop, M.D., Sc.D., is Surgeon General, Deputy Assistant Secretary for Health, and Director of the Office of International Health of the U.S. Public Health Service. A pediatric surgeon with an international reputation, he was previously surgeon-in-chief of Children's Hospital of Philadelphia and professor of pediatric surgery and pediatrics at the University of Pennsylvania. Dr. Koop is the author of more than 175 articles and books on the practice of medicine. He has served as surgery editor of the *Journal of Clinical Pediatrics* and editor-in-chief of the *Journal of Pediatric Surgery.* Dr. Koop has received nine honorary degrees and numerous other awards, including the Denis Brown Gold Medal of the British Association of Paediatric Surgeons, the William E. Ladd Gold Medal of the American Academy of Pediatrics, and the Copernicus Medal of the Surgical Society of Poland. He is a Chevalier of the French Legion of Honor and a member of the Royal College of Surgeons, London.